THE BAKER'S KITCHEN

★ *Easy, Impressive & Indulgent* ★

150

GREAT RECIPES

★

CONTENTS

INTRODUCTION

Is there a secret to good baking? Yes. The secret is that it's easier than you think! In this book, you will find 150 easy-to-follow recipes that will enable you to whip up fluffy scones for afternoon tea, bake awesome chocolate cakes for birthdays, dazzle at dinner parties with homemade breads and sumptuous desserts and keep the kids happy with healthy nut bars for their lunchboxes. It's all here and it's all doable. Follow the recipes in the pages of this book, and you'll be baking up a storm in no time. Here are a few notes to help you along.

BAKER'S NOTES

Weights and Measures

For ease of use, this book provides solid and liquid measurements in imperial and metric, and we've included cups too, which are standard use in Australian recipes. Note that cups are Australian cups and pints are American pints.

Temperature

Oven temperature is important in baking, but temperatures vary between ovens. Likewise, some ovens cook unevenly. Perhaps you have noticed one side getting more browned than the other in your oven. If that's the case, you'll need to rotate during baking. Get to know your own oven, so you know what adjustments to make to the temperature given in the recipe. If you want precision, invest in an oven thermometer.

Eggs

Unless otherwise specified, eggs should be brought up to room temperature before being used in baking. Remember that eggs come in different sizes. In this book, we have assumed large eggs (55g, 2oz). Be mindful of the size of eggs you are using and adjust as necessary.

Butter

We recommend using unsalted butter, unless a recipe states otherwise. Why? Well, one good reason is that then you can add salt to *your* taste. But, also, salted butter often contains a yellow food colouring called annatto, which you might prefer to avoid. And it has a higher water content than unsalted butter, meaning it may not fluff up quite so well on creaming.

When making cakes, butter generally needs to be softened to room temperature to allow it to cream together with sugar to create a light and fluffy mixture – the basis of many cakes.

When making pastry, butter may need to be chilled, allowing you to rub it with fingertips or cut it with a knife into the flour to create a crumble mixture – the basis of most pastries.

Chocolate

Where a recipe calls for dark chocolate, you can use bittersweet (65-70% cacoa) or semisweet (50-60% cacoa) or even unsweetened chocolate (up to 100% cacoa). The higher the cacoa content, the lower the sugar content, meaning the flavour is more chocolately and less sugary. If chocolate is the star in your dish, say in a ganache, buttercream frosting or chocolate tart then a higher cacoa content is a good choice. Milk chocolate is sweeter and may be used for pancakes, muffins or just to your taste preference. The best advice is to know your cacoa content (it's usually printed on the chocolate) and don't cook with anything you wouldn't be happy to eat.

Happy baking!

CAKES
AND
CUPCAKES

SERVES 12 ★ PREP 35MIN (PLUS CHILLING) ★ COOK TIME 25MIN

CHOCOLATE MINT CAKE

INGREDIENTS

Cake

1¾ cups (215g, 7oz) plain flour

¾ tsp bicarbonate of soda

½ tsp salt

110g (4oz) butter

1¾ cups (385g, 14oz) sugar

3 eggs

115g (4oz) chocolate, melted

1 tsp vanilla extract

¾ cup (185ml, 6fl oz) milk

½ cup (125ml, 4fl oz) water

Filling

1 cup (250ml, 8fl oz) thickened cream

3 tsps icing sugar

½ tsp peppermint extract

Icing

1 cup (170g, 6oz) chocolate chips

55g (2oz) butter

⅓ cup (80ml, 3fl oz) evapourated milk

1 tsp vanilla extract

1½ cups (235g, 8oz) icing sugar

Mint, to garnish

METHOD

1. Grease two 23cm (9in) round cake tins with greaseproof paper. Set aside.

2. Sift together the flour, bicarb and salt. Set aside.

3. In a large bowl or electric mixer, cream the butter and sugar until light and fluffy. Add eggs, one at a time, beating well after each addition. Combine the chocolate and vanilla and then add half to creamed mixture. Add milk and water, then add the other half of the chocolate mixture, beating well after each addition. Add in the flour mixture and fold through until well combined.

4. Pour into prepared tins. Bake at 180°C (350°F, Gas Mark 4) for 25 minutes or until a skewer comes out clean. Leave for 10 minutes before removing the cakes to cool on wire racks.

5. Meanwhile, to make the filling, beat the cream in a small bowl until it begins to thicken. Add icing sugar and peppermint extract and beat until stiff peaks form.

6. Place a cake layer on a serving plate. Spread with filling. Top with second cake layer.

7. To make the icing, melt chocolate chips and butter in a microwave or small saucepan over a low heat. Stir until smooth. Cool slightly. Beat in evapourated milk and vanilla extract. Gradually beat in icing sugar until smooth.

8. Frost cake. Chill for 1-2 hours before serving, garnished with sprigs of mint.

LEMON RING CAKE

INGREDIENTS

Cake

2½ cups (310g, 10oz) plain flour

2¼ tsps baking powder

½ tsp salt

4 eggs

2 cups (440g, 1lb) sugar

1 tsp vanilla extract

3 tbsps

2 tbsps lemon zest

1¼ cups (310ml, 10fl oz) milk

10 tbsps butter

METHOD

1. Preheat oven to 180°C (350°F, Gas Mark 4). Grease and lightly flour a bundt tin. Set aside.

2. Sieve flour, baking powder and salt in a small bowl and set aside.

3. Using an electric mixer, beat eggs on low until thick and pale yellow in color. Slowly add sugar and then increase to medium-high speed. Beat until light and fluffy. Stop mixer and stir in vanilla, lemon juice and lemon zest. Resume on low speed and add dry ingredients until combined to complete batter.

4. In a small saucepan, heat milk and butter until just melted. Add to batter and mix with a metal spoon until smooth.

5. Pour the batter into prepared tin and bake for 30 minutes or until a skewer inserted in the centre comes out clean.

6. Remove cake from oven and allow to cool in tin for 5 minutes. Turn cake onto a platter or cake stand.

BLACK FOREST GATEAU

INGREDIENTS

125g (4oz) butter

1½ cup (330g, 12oz) caster sugar

¼ cup (30g, 1oz) cocoa powder

½ tsp bicarbonate of soda

60g (2oz) dark chocolate, chopped

2 eggs

1½ cups (185g, 6oz) self-raising flour, sifted

2 tbsps arrowroot

Filling

1 x 400g (14oz) can sour cherries, drained, juice reserved

3 tsps arrowroot

1¼ cups (300ml, 10fl oz) thickened cream

3 tsps icing sugar

2 tbsps kirsch

Decoration

Flaked chocolate, to garnish

6-8 fresh cherries, to garnish

METHOD

1. Preheat the oven to 180°C (350°F, Gas Mark 4). Grease and line a deep 20cm (8in) springform cake tin.

2. Place butter, sugar, cocoa, bicarbonate of soda, chocolate and 1 cup (250ml, 8fl oz) water in a large saucepan over medium heat. Bring to the boil, stirring until melted. Reduce heat to low and cook for 3 minutes or until smooth and thickened. Set aside to cool slightly.

3. Stir the eggs, flour and arrowroot into the chocolate mixture, then pour into the tin.

4. Transfer to the oven and bake for 30 minutes or until a skewer inserted into the centre comes out clean. Cool slightly in the tin, then turn out onto a wire rack.

5. Place cherry juice in a small saucepan over medium heat. Dissolve the arrowroot in ¼ cup (60ml, 2fl oz) of cold water, then stir into the juice. Cook, stirring, for 2-3 minutes until thickened. Set aside to cool.

6. Whisk the cream and icing sugar with electric beaters until stiff peaks form.

7. Cut the cake horizontally into 4 layers. Place one cake layer on a serving plate, drizzle with kirsch and cherry syrup, then spread with whipped cream. Dot with sour cherries. Repeat layering of kirsch, cherry syrup, cream and sour cherries with the next two slices of cake, finishing with a cake layer.

8. Spread whipped cream over the cake and garnish with fresh cherries and flaked chocolate.

UPSIDE-DOWN PINEAPPLE CAKE

INGREDIENTS

Sauce

1 cup (155g, 5oz) dark brown sugar

110g (4oz) butter

1 x 400g (14oz) can pineapple slices

Cake

1½ cups (185g, 6oz) plain flour

2 tbsps cornflour

6 tbsps almond meal

¾ tsp baking powder

½ tsp salt

1¾ cups (385g, 14oz) sugar

225g (8oz) butter, room temperature

4 eggs

1 tsp vanilla extract

¾ cup (185ml, 6fl oz) sour cream

METHOD

1   Preheat the oven to 160°C (325°F, Gas Mark 3).

2. To make the caramel, place brown sugar and butter into a saucepan on a medium heat and cook for 3-5 minutes or until sugar dissolves and the mixture bubbles.

3. Pour caramel into a 25cm (10in) diameter cake tin with 5cm (2in) high sides. Arrange pineapple slices in a single layer on top of the caramel mixture in the tin.

4. Combine the flour, cornflour, almond meal, baking powder and salt in a large mixing bowl.

5. In a separate bowl, use an electric mixer to beat the sugar and butter together until light and fluffy. Add eggs one at a time, beating after each addition. Beat in the vanilla. Add half the dry ingredients and beat well. Add half the sour cream and beat well. Repeat this step with the remaining dry ingredients and sour cream. Pour cake batter over caramel and pineapple in tin.

6   Bake for 1 hour or until a skewer inserted into the centre comes out clean.

7. Remove and cool in the tin for 10 minutes. Turn cake out onto a platter and serve warm.

BATTENBERG CAKE

INGREDIENTS

170g (6oz) butter,
room temperature

¾ cup (165g, 6oz)
caster sugar

3 eggs

½ cup (60g, 2oz)
almond meal

1¼ cup (155g, 5oz)
self-raising flour

½ tsp baking powder

½ tsp almond extract

Pink food colouring

Topping

½ cup (180g, 6oz)
apricot jam

Icing sugar, for dusting

500g (1lb 2oz) white
marzipan

METHOD

1. Heat oven to 180°C (350°F, Gas Mark 4).

2. Take a 20cm (8in) square tin and place a double layer of foil to create a barrier in the centre (or use a Battenberg tin). Line each compartment with 2 pieces of baking paper.

3. Combine cake ingredients except food colouring in a large mixing bowl and blend with an electric mixer until smooth.

4. Tip half the batter into one side of the tin. Mix the pink food colouring into the remaining cake batter. Scrape the pink batter into the other side of the tin.

5. Transfer to the oven and bake for 30 minutes until a skewer inserted in the centre comes out clean.

6. Remove from oven and cool in the tin for 15 minutes, then transfer to a wire rack to cool completely.

7. Place cakes on top of each other and trim to level the sides and ensure perfect squares when assembled. Then cut each in half lengthways to create 2 pink and 2 plain rectangular sponges.

8. Heat apricot jam in a small pan then push through a sieve.

9. Sandwich the 2 pairs of sponges together like a checkerboard and spread jam over top and sides.

10. Place marzipan on a surface dusted with icing sugar and roll into a rectangle of about 40 x 20cm (16 x 10in), large enough to wrap the cake completely, leaving the ends exposed.

11. Turn the cake upside down on the marzipan and brush the underside of the sponges with jam. Wrap the marzipan around the cake, pressing it gently onto the surface of the sponges. Smooth it over the top and sides, and press edges together to join. Turn cake so the join is underneath. Trim a slice off each end to reveal the pink-and-white sponge.

ALMOND CAKE

INGREDIENTS

1½ cup (185g, 6oz)
whole almonds, toasted

4 eggs, separated

½ cup (180g, 6oz) honey

1 tsp vanilla extract

½ tsp bicarbonate
of soda

½ tsp salt

TOPPING

2 tbsps honey

¼ cup (40g, 1½ oz)
sliced almonds

METHOD

1. Preheat the oven to 180°C (350°F, Gas Mark 4). Grease a 23cm (9in) springform cake tin and line with greaseproof paper.

2. In a small frying pan over medium heat dry fry the sliced almonds for 3 minutes or until golden brown, stirring constantly. Set aside.

3. Process the whole almonds in a food processor or blender until finely ground.

4. In an electric mixer, beat 4 egg yolks, honey, vanilla, bicarb and salt in a large bowl on medium speed until well combined. Add the ground almonds and beat on low until combined.

5. In a separate bowl, beat 4 egg whites with the electric mixer on medium speed for 1-2 minutes until foamy, white and doubled in volume, but not stiff peaks.

6. Using a rubber spatula, gently fold the egg whites into the nut mixture until just combined. Scrape the batter into the prepared tin.

7. Bake the cake for 30 minutes or until golden brown and a skewer inserted in the centre comes out clean.

8. Allow the cake to cool in the tin for 10 minutes. Remove the side ring and cool completely.

9. Remove the cake from the tin bottom and carefully transfer to a serving platter. To serve, drizzle with honey and sprinkle with the toasted almonds.

PUMPKIN PECAN RING CAKE

INGREDIENTS

¾ cup (90g, 3oz) chopped pecans

1½ cups (240g, 8oz) packed brown sugar

55g (2oz) butter, room temperature

3 eggs

¾ cup (185ml, 6fl oz) vegetable oil

2 cups (450g,1lb) roasted pumpkin, pureed

2½ cups (310g, 10oz) plain flour

2 tsps baking powder

1¾ tsps ground cinnamon

1 tsp bicarbonate of soda

1 tsp ground ginger

¾ tsp salt

¼ tsp ground nutmeg

¼ tsp ground allspice

Syrup

55g (2oz) butter

⅔ cup (100g, 3oz) packed brown sugar

4 tbsps water

¼ cup (60ml, 2fl oz) dark rum (optional)

METHOD

1. Preheat oven to 180°C (350°F, Gas Mark 4) and line a cake ring tin with greaseproof paper.

2. Place pecans on baking tray and toast in the oven for 10 minutes. Remove and cool.

3. Mix cooled pecans with 2 tablespoons of brown sugar and sprinkle into the cake tin.

4. In large bowl or with an electric mixer, beat remaining sugar with butter until light. Add the eggs, one at a time, beating for 30 seconds each time. Add the oil and beat until fluffy. Beat in pumpkin until smooth.

5. In separate bowl, sift together flour, baking powder, cinnamon, bicarbonate of soda, ginger, salt, nutmeg and allspice. Stir into the egg mixture and fold together until well combined.

6. Transfer the mixture into the cake tin and place in the oven. Bake for 50 minutes or until a skewer inserted in centre comes out clean.

7. Remove from the oven and allow to cool in the tin for 10 minutes. Remove from the tin and place on a wire rack to cool thoroughly.

8. In small saucepan, melt butter over medium heat. Stir in sugar and water. Increase heat and boil for 3 minutes or until sugar has dissolved and syrup has thickened. Stir in rum, if using. Brush syrup over cooled cake.

BUTTERFLY CAKES

INGREDIENTS

110g (4oz) butter,
room temperature

¾ cup (165g, 6oz)
caster sugar

1 tsp vanilla paste

2 eggs

1½ cups (185g, 6oz)
self-raising flour,
sifted

½ cup (125ml, 4fl oz)
milk

1¼ cups (310ml, 10fl oz)
thickened cream

1 tbsp caster sugar

⅓ cup (115g, 4oz)
strawberry jam

Icing sugar, to finish

METHOD

1. Preheat oven to 180°C (350°F, Gas Mark 4), and place 12 large muffin liners into muffin tray.

2. Using an electric mixer, cream butter, sugar and vanilla until light and fluffy.

3. Add eggs one at a time, and beat after each addition until smooth. Stir in half the flour and half the milk. Repeat with remaining milk and flour and fold mixture until well incorporated.

4. Spoon batter into muffin liners, filling two-thirds of the way. Place in the oven and bake for 15 minutes, or until skewer comes out clean.

5. Remove from oven and cool completely. Cut a circle from the top of each cake and set circles aside.

6. Whip the thickened cream with sugar to form stiff peaks. Fill each cake with a small dollop of jam then the cream mix.

7. Cut the cake circles in half and arrange on cupcakes to form wings. Dust with icing sugar to serve.

CHOCOLATE LAYER CAKE

INGREDIENTS

Cake

1½ cups (330g, 12oz) sugar

1¼ cups (155g, 5oz) plain flour, sifted

¾ cup (90g, 3oz) unsweetened cocoa powder

2½ tsps baking powder

1½ tsps bicarbonate of soda

⅛ tsp salt

1 cup (250ml, 8fl oz) buttermilk

3 large eggs

2 tsps vanilla extract

8 tbsps butter

Frosting

500g (1lb 2oz) dark chocolate, finely chopped

1 cup (250ml, 8fl oz) thickened cream

2 tbsps sugar

6 tbsps butter

Sugar syrup

1 tbsp sugar

1 tbsp water

Chocolate flakes, to decorate

METHOD

1. Preheat the oven to 160°C (325°F, Gas Mark 3). Line the bottom of three 20cm (8in) round cake tins with greaseproof paper.

2. In a large mixing bowl, combine the sugar, flour, cocoa powder, baking powder, bicarbonate of soda and salt.

3. In a small bowl, whisk buttermilk, eggs and vanilla.

4. Melt the butter in a small pan over medium heat.

5. Using an electric mixer, beat half the buttermilk mixture into the dry ingredients at low speed. Add half the butter and beat for 30 seconds. Add the remaining buttermilk and butter and beat until combined.

6. Pour the batter evenly into the tins and bake for 30 minutes until a skewer inserted in the centre comes out clean. Cool in the tins for 10 minutes, then turn out onto a rack to cool completely. Remove greaseproof paper.

7. For the frosting, put the chocolate in a large bowl. In a small saucepan, bring cream and sugar to a boil. Pour cream over the chocolate and leave to stand for 5 minutes. Gently whisk until smooth. Add the butter and whisk until incorporated. Refrigerate for 30 minutes or until thick enough to spread.

8. For the syrup, combine the sugar and water in a small saucepan over medium-high heat. Allow to bubble until the sugar has dissolved.

9. Set a cake layer on a plate and brush with sugar syrup. Spread a layer of frosting on top. Repeat with the other 2 cake layers. Finish by spreading the remaining frosting around the sides of the cake. Decorate with chocolate flakes.

CHRISTMAS FRUIT CAKE

INGREDIENTS

250g (9oz) butter

1kg (2lb) mixed dried fruit

1½ cups (235g, 8oz) brown sugar, firmly packed

½ cup (125ml, 4fl oz) brandy

½ cup (125ml, 4fl oz) water

½ tsp bicarbonate of soda

2 tsps orange rind, grated

1 tsp lemon rind, grated

⅓ cup (40g, 1½ oz) walnuts, chopped

450g (1lb) treacle

5 eggs, beaten

2 cups (250g, 8oz) plain flour

½ cup (60g, 2oz) self-raising flour

METHOD

1. Preheat oven to 140°C (285°F, Gas Mark 1) and line a deep 23cm (9in) round cake tin, at the base and sides to 5cm (2in) above edge of tin.

2. Place butter, fruit, sugar, brandy and water in a large saucepan over a high heat and bring to the boil. Stir well and then reduce heat and simmer, covered, for 10 minutes.

3. Add bicarb then stir, cover and allow to cool.

4. Add rinds, walnuts, treacle, eggs and flours to cooled mixture and stir well to combine. Spread evenly into prepared tin.

5. Place in the oven and bake for 2¾ hours.

6. When cooked remove from the oven and cover tightly with foil. Allow to cool in tin.

VANILLA CUPCAKES

INGREDIENTS

Cupcakes

150g (5oz) butter,
room temperature

1½ cups (330g, 12oz)
caster sugar

2 eggs

2½ cups (310g, 10oz)
self-raising flour

1¼ cups (310ml, 10fl oz)
milk

2 tsps vanilla essence

Icing

100g (3½ oz) butter,
room temperature

1½ cups (235g, 8oz)
icing sugar

2 drops vanilla essence

2 tbsps milk

METHOD

1. Preheat oven to 190°C (375°F, Gas Mark 5). Place paper cases in a muffin tray.

2. Using an electric mixer, beat butter until smooth, add caster sugar and beat well until light and fluffy. Add eggs and beat. Add the sifted flour, milk and vanilla and stir until a smooth batter forms. Spoon mixture into the cases to about a third full.

3. Bake for 20 minutes until golden or until springy to touch. Turn out onto a wire rack to cool while you prepare the icing.

4. In an electric mixer, beat butter until it is pale and fluffy. Sift over the icing sugar and add the vanilla essence and milk. Beat until the mixture has a light, fluffy texture. Add extra milk for a softer consistency. Spread or pipe icing over cupcakes and top with decorations as desired.

SERVES 6-8 ★ PREP 20MIN ★ COOK TIME 1HR

CHOCOLATE HAZELNUT CAKE

INGREDIENTS

Cake

250g (9oz) butter

225g (8oz, ½ lb) milk
cooking chocolate, chopped

5 eggs

1½ cups (235g, 8oz)
brown sugar

1 cup (125g, 4oz)
plain flour, sifted

50g (2oz) ground
hazelnut meal

Sauce

½ cup (125ml, 4fl oz)
thickened cream

200g (7oz) dark cooking
chocolate, chopped

Chopped hazelnuts,
to decorate

METHOD

1. Preheat oven to 180°C (350°F, Gas Mark 4). Line a 20cm (8in) square cake tin with greaseproof paper.

2. Melt butter and milk chocolate together in a small pan over low heat, stirring until smooth. Remove from heat.

3. Using a hand beater or electric mixer, whisk eggs and brown sugar together lightly. Add chocolate mixture and stir to combine. Combine flour and hazelnut meal and fold gently into chocolate mixture. Pour mixture into prepared tin.

4. Bake for 1 hour or until a skewer inserted in the centre comes out clean. Remove from oven and cool in tin for 10 minutes. Turn out onto a wire rack to cool completely.

5. Heat cream in a small pan until it just starts to bubble at the edges. Remove from heat and add dark chocolate. Stir until chocolate has melted. Cool until the sauce begins to thicken.

6. Place cake on a wire rack over a tray or board to catch the drips. Pour chocolate sauce over cake and smooth with a spatula. Sprinkle with chopped nuts. Leave to set before serving.

HUMMINGBIRD CAKE

INGREDIENTS

Cake

2 x 225g (8oz) cans pineapple in juice

3 cups (375g, 12oz) plain flour

2 tsps baking powder

1 tsp bicarbonate of soda

1 tsp ground cinnamon

1 tsp salt

2 cups (440g, 1lb) sugar

3 eggs

1 cup (250ml, 8fl oz) vegetable oil

4 ripe bananas, mashed

1½ cups (210g, 7oz) pecans, toasted, chopped

2 tsps vanilla extract

Frosting

280g (10oz) butter, room temperature

4 cups (620g, 1lb 4 oz) icing sugar

2½ tsps vanilla extract

½ tsp salt

500g (1lb 2oz) cream cheese, cut into pieces

½ cup (60g, 2oz) pecans, toasted and chopped

METHOD

1. Preheat oven to 180°C (350°F, Gas Mark 4) and line two 23cm (9in) round cake tins. Set aside.

2. Put pineapple in a fine-mesh strainer over a small saucepan, pressing to remove juice. Place saucepan on medium heat and cook juice for 5 minutes or until reduced to 1 cup (250ml, 8fl oz). Set aside.

3. In a medium bowl, combine flour, baking powder, bicarbonate of soda, cinnamon and salt. Set aside.

4. Whisk sugar and eggs together in a large bowl. Add oil and whisk. Add bananas, pecans, vanilla, drained pineapple flesh and pineapple juice and mix well. Gently stir in the flour mixture until just combined.

5. Divide the batter evenly between the cake tins. Bake for 50 minutes or until deep golden brown on top and a skewer inserted in the centre comes out clean.

6. Let the cakes cool in tins on a wire rack for 20 minutes, then turn out of the tins, and allow to cool completely on a wire rack.

7. Using an electric mixer, beat the butter, sugar, vanilla and salt on low speed until smooth. Increase speed to medium-low and add the cream cheese one piece at a time and mix until smooth.

8. To assemble, place one cake on a plate. Spread a layer of frosting over top, then add the second cake layer, pressing lightly. Spread another layer of frosting over the top of the cake. Spread the remaining frosting evenly over the sides of the cake. Top the cake with the chopped pecans. Refrigerate before serving.

PANFORTE

INGREDIENTS

5 tbsps unsweetened cocoa powder

2½ cups (325g) mixed nuts (pistachios, almonds or hazelnuts), toasted

1 cup (125g, 4oz) plain flour

1 cup (170g) dried cranberries, chopped

1 cup (170g) dried figs, chopped

1 tbsp ground cinnamon

2 tsps ground ginger

Pinch of grated nutmeg

½ tsp chilli powder (optional)

90g (3oz) dark chocolate, chopped

1 cup (220g, 8oz) sugar

¾ cup (260g, 9oz) honey

extra cocoa powder, for lining and dusting

METHOD

1. Preheat the oven to 160°C (325°F, Gas Mark 3) and grease and line a large baking tin. Dust the inside (base and sides) with cocoa powder.

2. In a large bowl, mix together the cocoa powder, nuts, flour, dried fruit, cinnamon, ginger, nutmeg, and chilli powder, if using.

3. Melt the chocolate in a small heatproof bowl set over a pan of simmering water. Set aside when just melted.

4. Heat the sugar and honey in a saucepan over a medium-high heat until completely dissolved and the syrup has thickened.

5. Pour the hot syrup over the nut mixture. Add the melted chocolate, and stir to combine.

6. Scrape the batter into the prepared tin and carefully smooth the surface with a spatula.

7. Transfer to the oven and bake for 40 minutes until set but still just soft in the centre.

8. Transfer to a wire rack to cool for 15 minutes, then remove from the tin to cool completely.

9. Dust with cocoa powder to serve.

RED VELVET CUPCAKES

INGREDIENTS

Cupcakes

2 cups (250g, 8oz) plain flour

2 tbsps cocoa powder

½ tsp salt

1⅓ cups (290g, 10½ oz) sugar

1¼ cups (325ml, 11fl oz) vegetable oil

2 eggs

1 tsp vanilla extract

2 tbsps red food colouring

1 cup (250ml, 8fl oz) buttermilk

2 tbsps white vinegar

1½ tsps bicarbonate of soda

Cream Cheese Frosting

230g (8oz) cream cheese, room temperature

115g (4oz) butter, room temperature

¾ cup (120g, 4oz) icing sugar

2 tbsps strawberry extract

METHOD

1. Preheat oven to 180°C (350°F, Gas Mark 4)°C and line 12 muffin cups with paper liners.

2. In a large bowl sift together flour, cocoa powder and salt. Set aside.

3. Using an electric mixer on medium speed, beat sugar and vegetable oil together. Add eggs one at a time, mixing well after each addition. Add vanilla extract and red food colouring and mix to combine. Gradually add dry ingredients to the bowl, alternating with the buttermilk. Mix well after each addition.

4. Combine vinegar and bicarbonate of soda in a small bowl. Stir well until the mixture bubbles slightly. Add into the batter and stir to combine.

5. Spoon mixture into muffin cups three-quarters of the way.

6. Place in the oven and bake for 20 minutes or until a skewer inserted into the centre comes out clean. Cool on a wire rack before frosting. Reserve one cupcake and crumble into a bowl.

7. Using an electric mixer, cream together the cream cheese and butter until light and fluffy. Slowly add the icing sugar until incorporated. Add the strawberry extract and mix well

8. Pipe the frosting on top of the cupcakes in a spiral shape. Decorate with the reserved cupcake crumbs.

CHOCOLATE ROULADE WITH COFFEE CREAM

INGREDIENTS

Cake

¼ cup (30g, 1oz) plain flour

2 tbsps cocoa powder

2 tbsps cornflour

½ tsp ground cinnamon

½ tsp baking powder

¼ tsp bicarbonate of soda

2 tsps instant coffee

4 eggs, separated

¾ cup (165g, 6oz) sugar

½ tsp almond extract

Filling

½ cup (110g, 4oz) sugar

3 tbsps cornflour

1 tbsp instant coffee

1 cup (250ml, 8fl oz) milk

2 egg yolks

1 tsp gelatin powder

1 tbsp butter

1 tsp vanilla

¾ cup (185ml, 6fl oz) cream

METHOD

1. Heat oven to 180°C (350°F, Gas Mark 4) and line a baking tray with greaseproof paper.

2. Sift together flour, cocoa powder, cornflour, cinnamon, baking powder and bicarbonate of soda. Set aside. Dissolve coffee in 1 teaspoon very hot water in small cup. Set aside.

3. In an electric mixer, beat egg whites at high speed until soft. Gradually beat in ½ cup (110g, 4oz) sugar until stiff peaks form. Set aside.

4. Beat together ¼ cup (55g, 2oz) sugar and yolks for 5 minutes until ribbons form when mixture is lifted. Add coffee and almond extract and beat for 2 minutes. Stir beaten whites into yolk mixture. Add flour mixture and fold gently. Turn into prepared tray, spreading evenly.

5. Bake for 15 minutes. To unmould, cover cake with a clean kitchen towel and invert. Remove tray, then paper. Trim the long sides of cake to create a clean edge. Starting from a short end, roll up cake using the towel. Cool, seam side down, on wire rack.

6. Put sugar, cornflour and coffee in a medium-sized saucepan. Whisk in milk and egg yolks. Bring to boil, stirring until thick. Remove from heat. Whisk in gelatin, butter and vanilla. Scrape into small bowl and place this bowl in larger bowl of ice water. Let stand, whisking frequently, until well chilled, about 5 minutes.

7. Beat cream until stiff peaks start to form. Fold into cooled coffee custard. Unroll cake and spread filling over. Reroll cake and place on platter. Decorate, if desired. Refrigerate at least 1 hour or until set.

MARBLE CAKE

INGREDIENTS

225g (8oz, ½ lb) butter, room temperature

1 cup (225g, 8oz) caster sugar

4 eggs

2 cups (225g, 8oz) self-raising flour

3 tbsps milk

1½ tsps vanilla extract

2 tbsps cocoa powder

METHOD

1. Heat oven to 180°C (350°F, Gas Mark 4). Grease a 20cm (8in) cake tin and line the bottom with greaseproof paper.

2. Using an electric mixer, beat the butter and sugar together until light and fluffy, then add the eggs, one at a time, mixing well after each addition. Fold through the flour, milk and vanilla extract until the mixture is smooth.

3. Divide the mixture into two bowls. Stir the cocoa powder into the mixture in one of the bowls. Dollop the chocolate and vanilla cake mixture into the tin alternately. Take a skewer or fork and swirl it around the mixture in the tin a few times to create a marbled effect.

4. Bake for 50 mins until a skewer inserted into the centre of the cake comes out clean. Turn out onto a cooling rack and leave to cool.

SERVES 8 ★ PREP 25MIN ★ COOK TIME 45MIN

ORANGE ALMOND CAKE

INGREDIENTS

1 orange, plus zest

3 eggs

1 cup (220g, 8oz)
caster sugar

2½ cups (300g, 10oz)
almond meal

½ tsp baking powder

METHOD

1. Preheat the oven to 150°C (300°F, Gas Mark 2) and line a 20cm (8in) round cake tin with greaseproof paper.

2. Place orange in a small saucepan, cover with water and boil for 10 minutes. Remove the orange and allow to cool. Peel and remove the seeds. Puree the flesh in a food processor or blender then pass through a sieve using the back of a metal spoon. Set aside the juice and discard the pulp.

3. Beat the eggs and sugar together in large bowl until pale and thick. Add the almond meal, baking powder, orange juice and zest and mix well to combine.

4. Spoon into tin and bake for 45 minutes, or until the top is springy to touch and golden brown.

5. Cool in the tin for 5 minutes before turning out on a wire rack.

APPLE CINNAMON CAKE

INGREDIENTS

Cake

2 eggs, separated

¾ cup (120g, 4oz) caster sugar

1¾ cups (215g, 7oz) self-raising flour, sifted

¾ cup (185ml, 6fl oz) milk

6 tbsps butter, melted

½ tsp vanilla extract

1 apple, cored, sliced

Topping

10g (¼ oz) butter, melted

1 tbsp caster sugar

½ tsp ground cinnamon

METHOD

1. Preheat oven to 190°C (375°F, Gas Mark 5). Line a 20cm (8in) cake tin with greaseproof paper.

2. Using an electric mixer, beat egg whites until soft peaks form. Gradually add sugar beating constantly, until mixture is thick and glossy. Beat in egg yolks.

3. Using a large metal spoon, gently fold through flour alternately with combination of milk, butter and vanilla extract. Finish the process by folding in flour.

4. Pour into prepared tin and arrange apple slices on top. Bake for 30-35 minutes, until a skewer inserted in the centre comes out clean.

5. Brush hot cake with melted butter and sprinkle with combined sugar and cinnamon. Cut and serve warm.

COFFEE AND WALNUT CAKE

INGREDIENTS

Cake

50g (2oz) walnut pieces

1 cup (220g, 8oz) aster sugar

225g (8oz, ½ lb) butter, room temperature

1¾ cups (215g, 7oz) plain flour

4 tsps instant coffee

2½ tsps baking powder

½ tsp bicarbonate of soda

4 eggs

1-2 tbsps milk

Filling

2 cups (310g, 10oz) icing sugar

175g (6oz) butter, room temperature

2 tsps instant coffee (dissolved in 1 tbsp boiling water)

5 walnuts, halved, to decorate

METHOD

1. Preheat the oven to 180°C (350°F, Gas Mark 4) and line two 20cm (8in) cake tins with greaseproof paper.

2. Pulse the walnut pieces and sugar in a food processor to a fine powder.

3. Add the rest of the cake ingredients except for milk and process to a smooth batter.

4. Add the milk, pouring it down the side of the bowl with the motor still running on slow speed. Add more milk if needed to achieve a soft consistency where mixture drops off a spoon.

5. Divide the mixture between the tins and bake in the oven for 25 minutes, or until springy to the touch.

6. Cool cakes in their tins for 10 minutes, then turn out onto a wire rack and remove greaseproof paper.

7. Sift icing sugar into the food processor, then add butter and process to make a smooth icing.

8. Add the hot coffee mixture processor, pulsing to blend into the buttercream.

9. To assemble, place one sponge with the flat base on a serving plate. Spread half the icing over the sponge with a spatula and then place the second sponge on top. Smooth the buttercream on top with a spatula. Decorate with walnuts.

CHOCOLATE CUPCAKES

INGREDIENTS

Cake

2 cups (250g, 8oz) plain flour, sifted

½ cup (60g, 2oz) cocoa powder, sifted

1 cup (220g, 8oz) sugar

1 tsp bicarbonate of soda

½ tsp of salt

½ cup (125ml, 4fl oz) oil

1 cup (250ml, 8fl oz) water

1 tsp vanilla extract

1 tbsp vinegar

Icing

125g (4oz) dark chocolate, chopped

150g (5oz) butter, room temperature

1¹/₃ cup (195g, 7oz) icing sugar

1 tsp vanilla extract

Chocolate sprinkles, to decorate

METHOD

1. Preheat the oven to 180°C (350°F, Gas Mark 4) and line a muffin tray with muffin liners.

2. Prepare two mixing bowls. Combine the dry ingredients in one and the wet ingredients in the other.

3. Using a metal spoon gently stir the wet ingredients into the dry ingredients until well combined.

4. Pour batter into muffin cups, filling to two-thirds of the way.

5. Place in the oven and bake for 20 minutes. When springy to touch, remove and cool on a wire rack. Cool completely.

6. Put the chocolate in a heatproof bowl and place bowl in a saucepan of simmering water. Melt the chocolate and set aside until it cools to room temperature.

7. Using an electric mixer, beat the butter until smooth and soft. Add the sugar and beat again until light and fluffy. Add the vanilla extract and melted chocolate. Beat the mixture again until shiny and smooth.

8. Transfer chocolate icing to a piping bag and pipe onto the cupcakes in a spiral. Decorate with chocolate sprinkles.

EASY CARROT CAKE

INGREDIENTS

Cake

1 cup (125g, 4oz)
self-raising flour

½ cup (60g, 2oz)
plain flour

1 tsp bicarbonate
of soda

½ tsp cinnamon

3 carrots, grated

½ cup (60g, 2oz) walnuts,
roughly chopped

½ cup (80g, 3oz)
brown sugar

¾ cup (185ml, 6fl oz)
olive oil

½ cup (180g, 6oz)
golden syrup

3 eggs, lightly beaten

1 tsp vanilla extract

Icing

250g (9oz) cream
cheese, chopped
into pieces

½ cup (80g, 3oz)
icing sugar

1 tsp vanilla extract

½ cup (60g, 2oz)
chopped walnuts,
to finish

METHOD

1. Preheat oven to 160°C (325°F, Gas Mark 3) and line a 24cm (9½ in) springform cake tin with greaseproof paper.

2. In a large bowl, combine together flours, bicarb and cinnamon. Stir through the carrots and walnuts.

3. In a separate bowl, combine brown sugar, oil, syrup, eggs and vanilla. Pour the wet ingredients into the dry and stir until just combined.

4. Pour mixture into tin and bake for 1 hour, 15 minutes, or until dark golden and firm to the touch. Remove from the oven and cool for 10 minutes before removing to a wire rack to cool completely.

5. Combine cream cheese, icing sugar and vanilla in the bowl of an electric mixer. Beat until light and fluffy.

6. When cake has cooled, smooth on the icing with a spatula and sprinkle with chopped walnuts.

LAMINGTONS

INGREDIENTS

Cake

2 cups (250g, 8oz) plain flour

4 tsps baking powder

Pinch of salt

125g (4oz) butter

¾ cup (165g, 6oz) white sugar

1 tsp vanilla essence

2 eggs

½ cup (125ml, 4fl oz) milk

Icing

4 cups (620g, 1lb 4 oz) icing sugar

⅓ cup (35g, 1oz) cocoa

½ cup (125ml, 4fl oz) milk

2 tbsps butter

500g (1lb 2oz) desiccated coconut for rolling

METHOD

1. Preheat oven to 190°C (375°F, Gas Mark 5) and line a deep-sided 30cm (12in) rectangular cake tin.

2. Sift together flour, baking powder and salt. Set aside.

3. Using an electric mixer, cream butter, sugar and vanilla essence until light and fluffy.

4. Add the eggs one at a time, beating well after each addition. Add half of the flour mixture and half of the milk and beat well. Repeat with remaining milk and flour.

5. Pour mixture into cake tin and bake for 35 minutes or until a skewer inserted into the centre of the cake comes out clean.

6. Remove from oven and allow to stand for 5 minutes, then turn out onto a wire rack and cool completely.

7. Combine icing sugar and cocoa in a large mixing bowl. Heat milk and butter in a saucepan until the butter is melted. Add to the sugar mixture and mix well to create a liquid icing that is not too watery.

8. Scatter coconut evenly in the base of a shallow container.

9. Prepare a wire rack with a board or baking paper underneath to catch any drips.

10. Cut the cake into squares. Using tongs or a fork, dip each square completely into the icing, then roll in the coconut. Repeat until all cake squares have been finished.

EASTER CAKE

INGREDIENTS

Cake

175g (6oz) butter, room temperature

1 cup (175g, 6oz) light muscovado sugar

3 eggs

1½ cups (185g, 6oz) self-raising flour

1 cup (160g, 6oz) sultanas

½ cup (80g, 3oz) currants

½ cup (80g, 3oz) glacé cherries, quartered

¼ cup (40g, 1½ oz) candied peel, roughly chopped

1 lemon, zested

1 tsp ground mixed spice

Decoration

500g (1lb 2oz) marzipan

2 tbsps apricot jam

1 egg white

METHOD

1. Preheat oven to 150°C (300°F, Gas Mark 2) and line an 18cm (7in) springform cake tin with greaseproof paper.

2. Roll out two-thirds of the almond paste. Cut two rounds, using the base of the cake tin as a guide. Roll the final third and form into 12 egg-shaped balls. Set aside.

3. Place all of the cake ingredients in the bowl of an electric mixer and beat until thoroughly combined.

4. Spoon half the cake mixture into the tin and smooth over. Add a round of almond paste and then spoon over the remaining cake mixture. Level the surface.

5. Place in the centre of the oven and bake for 2 hours until golden and firm to the touch.

6. Remove from the oven and leave to cool in the tin for 10 minutes, before removing from tin and placing on a wire rack to cool completely.

7. Warm the jam in a small saucepan and brush over the top of the cake. Put a round of marzipan on top of the jam and crimp the edges using a spoon.

8. Take the prepared almond balls and brush with egg white. Place under a hot grill for 1-2 minutes, until golden. When cool, place around the edge of the cake, attaching with a dab of egg white.

RAW CARROT CAKE WITH CASHEW CREAM

INGREDIENTS

Cake

2 large carrots, diced

1½ cups (240g, 8oz) oat or buckwheat flour

1 cup (140g, 5oz) dates

1 cup (140g, 5oz) dried pineapple

½ cup (80g, 3oz) dried coconut

½ tsp cinnamon

Frosting

2 cups (280g, 10oz) cashews, soaked for 2 hours

1-2 tbsps lemon juice

2 tbsps coconut oil

⅓ cup (80ml, 3fl oz) maple syrup

Water, as needed

Cashew nuts and dried cranberries, chopped, to decorate

METHOD

1. Place all the cake ingredients in a food processor and pulse until coarsely chopped and a dough-like consistency forms. Set aside.

2. Place all the frosting ingredients in a high speed blender and blend until smooth, adding a small amount of water, just enough to hold the frosting together.

3. Press half the cake mix into the bottom of a springform tin. Then spread over a generous layer of the frosting. Put in the freezer for 30 minutes or until the layer of frosting is hard.

4. Remove from freezer and press on the rest of the cake mix. Remove cake from the tin. Spread remaining frosting on the top and sides of the cake. Scatter with cashews and cranberries. Refrigerate until ready to eat.

ZESTY ORANGE BUTTER CAKE

INGREDIENTS

125g (4oz) butter, room temperature

¼ cup (60ml, 2fl oz) milk

¼ cup (60ml, 2fl oz) orange juice

2 eggs

¾ cup (165g, 6oz) caster sugar

2 cups (250g, 8oz) self-raising flour, sifted

1 tbsp orange zest

METHOD

1   Preheat oven to 180°C (350°F, Gas Mark 4) and line a 20cm (8in) deep cake tin with greaseproof paper.

2. Using an electric mixer, combine all cake ingredients in a large bowl and beat thoroughly until well mixed.

3. Pour cake mixture into tin and place in oven. Bake for 35 minutes until a skewer inserted in the centre comes out clean.

4   Turn onto wire rack and allow to cool.

5   Dust with icing sugar

ORANGE UPSIDE-DOWN SYRUP CAKE

INGREDIENTS

Syrup

1 cup (220g, 8oz) caster sugar

½ cup (125ml, 4fl oz) water

1 vanilla bean, seeds scraped

2 oranges, thinly sliced

Cake

4 eggs

1 cup (220g, 8oz) caster sugar

1 tsp vanilla extract

1¼ cups (155g, 5oz) self-raising flour

150g (5oz) butter, melted

1 cup (130g, 4½ oz) almond meal

METHOD

1. Preheat oven to 160°C (325°F, Gas Mark 3) and line a 23cm (9in) deep-sided springform cake tin with greaseproof paper.

2. Place sugar, water and vanilla in a large saucepan over medium heat. Heat, stirring constantly, for 5 minutes or until sugar is dissolved. Add oranges and simmer for 10 minutes until soft. Remove from the heat and set aside to cool slightly.

3. When orange is slightly cooled, transfer the orange mixture to the cake tin.

4. Meanwhile, place eggs, sugar and vanilla in the bowl of an electric mixer and beat thoroughly until mixture is thick, pale and increased in volume. This may take up to 10 minutes.

5. Sift flour over the egg mixture and fold through with a metal spoon. Next fold through butter and almond meal.

6. Pour cake mixture over the orange and bake for 45 minutes or until a skewer inserted in the centre comes out clean.

7. Remove from oven and allow to cool slighly. Turn out onto a platter to serve warm.

CAKE POPS

INGREDIENTS

1 chocolate cake

225g (8oz, ½ lb) cream cheese, room temperature

4 tbsps butter

2 cups (310g, 10oz) icing sugar

1 tbsp milk (or more, as necessary)

Cake pop or lollipop sticks

345g (12oz) chocolate chips

345g (12oz) white chocolate chips

Food colouring, as required

Colored sugars, candies, and other decorative sprinkles

METHOD

1. Break the cake into a large bowl and crumble with fingers or a fork to a breadcrumb consistency.

2. In a separate bowl, whip the cream cheese, butter, icing sugar and milk together until smooth. Scrape into bowl with cake crumbs and mix with with fingers until fully incorporated. Add additional milk, as required, until the mixture will hold together when rolled into a ball.

3. Roll all the mixture into balls and insert sticks. Place in the freezer for about 20 minutes.

4. When ready to prepare the cake pops, melt the chocolate. Place chocolate and white chocolate in separate heatproof bowls over a pan of simmering water on a medium heat (or melt chocolate in microwave).

5. For pink or other coloured chocolate, add a few drops of food colouring to the white chocolate.

6. Prepare decorations by sprinkling them onto pieces of greaseproof paper.

7. Dip the cake pops into the chocolate and fully submerge.

8. Let the excess chocolate drip off. Swirl and tap gently if needed.

9. Roll the cake pop in sprinkles and other decorations as desired.

CHOCOLATE MUD CAKE

INGREDIENTS

Cake

2 cups (440g, 1lb)
caster sugar

1½ cups (185g, 6oz)
plain flour

¼ cup (30g, 1oz)
self-raising flour

¼ cup (30g, 1oz)
cocoa

250g (9oz) butter,
chopped coarsely

200g (7oz) dark
chocolate, chopped
coarsely

1⅓ cups (330ml,
11fl oz) milk

1 tsp vanilla extract

2 eggs

Ganache

⅓ cup (80ml, 3fl oz)
cream

200g (7oz) dark
chocolate chips

1 cup (155g, 5oz) milk
chocolate chips, to
decorate

METHOD

1. Preheat oven to 170°C (340°F, Gas Mark 4). Line a deep 22cm (8½in) round cake tin with greaseproof paper.

2. Sift the dry ingredients together in a large bowl. Set aside.

3. Place butter, chocolate, milk and vanilla extract in a medium saucepan over low heat and stir until mixture is smooth.

4. Cool mixture until barely warm. Add sifted dry ingredients and eggs and whisk with a hand whisk or electric hand mixer.

5. Pour mixture into tin and place in the oven to bake 1½ hours.

6. Heat the cream in a small saucepan over medium heat until it just begins to bubble at the edge. Remove from heat, add the chocolate chips and stir until smooth and well combined. Refrigerate ganache for 30 minutes.

7. Remove cake from oven and allow to cool in tin for 5 minutes before turning onto a wire rack to cool completely.

8. Remove ganache from the fridge. Beat with a metal spoon until smooth and spread over cake. Decorate with milk chocolate chips.

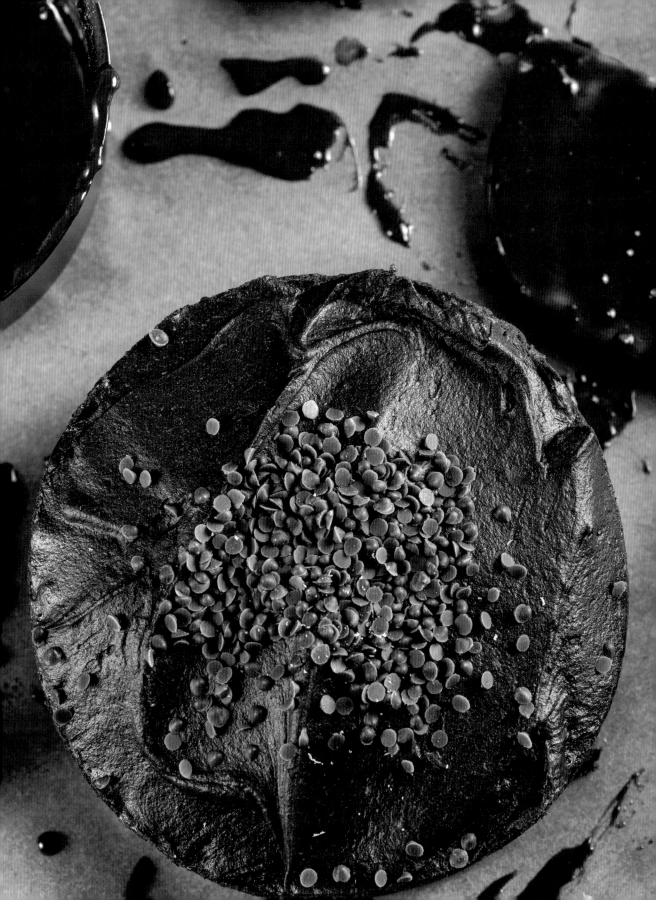

VICTORIA SPONGE CAKE

INGREDIENTS

Cake

175g (6oz) butter,
room temperature

¾ cup (175g, 6oz)
caster sugar

3 fresh eggs

1½ cup (175g, 6oz)
self-raising flour

Filling

1 cup (200g, 7oz)
strawberries

2 cups (200g, 7oz)
blueberries

1 cup (250ml, 8fl oz)
thickened cream

1 tbsp icing sugar
and extra for dusting

1 tsp vanilla bean paste,
or vanilla extract

4 tbsps strawberry jam

METHOD

1. Preheat the oven to 180°C (350°F, Gas Mark 4) and line two 18cm (7in) sandwich tins with greaseproof paper.

2. In an electric mixer, cream the butter and the sugar until pale and fluffy. Add the eggs, one at a time, beating well after each addition. Gradually fold in the flour until incorporated.

3. Divide the mixture evenly between the tins and bake in the oven for 20 minutes until golden brown and springy to the touch.

4. Remove from the oven and cool the sponge cakes in tins for 5 minutes before transferring to a wire rack to cool completely.

5. Hull the strawberries and slice them in half.

6. In an electric mixer, whip the cream until almost stiff peaks, then mix in icing sugar and vanilla.

7. To assemble, spread jam on one of the sponge cakes and spread whipped cream on top. Place half of the strawberries and blueberries on top of the cream. Place the other sponge cake on top and dust with icing sugar.

SLICES
AND
BISCUITS

OATMEAL RAISIN COOKIES

INGREDIENTS

²/₃ cup (100g, 3½ oz) raisins

²/₃ cup (160ml, 5fl oz) vegetable oil

1 cup (220g, 8oz) caster sugar

1 egg, beaten

1 tsp ground cinnamon

1 tsp vanilla extract

1¼ cups (155g, 5oz) plain flour

¼ tsp bicarbonate of soda

Pinch of salt

300g (10oz) oats

METHOD

1. Heat the oven to 180°C (350°F, Gas Mark 4) and line two baking trays with greaseproof paper.

2. Cover the raisins with boiling water and leave to soak for 20 mins until plump. Drain, reserving the liquid.

3. In a large bowl, mix together oil and sugar. Gradually beat in the egg and the add cinnamon, vanilla extract and the water from the raisins. Sift the flour, bicarbonate of soda and a pinch of salt into the bowl. Add the oats and stir. Finally, mix in the raisins and stir until well combined.

4. Drop heaped tablespoons of the dough onto baking trays, spaced apart to allow for spread when cooking. Bake for 15 minutes until golden. Leave to cool on the trays for 10 minutes then transfer to a wire rack to cool completely

5. Store in an airtight container for up to 3 days.

CLASSIC SHORTBREAD

INGREDIENTS

125g (4oz) butter

¼ cup (55g, 2oz) caster sugar plus extra to dust

1½ cups (185g, 6oz) plain flour

icing sugar, to dust

METHOD

1. Preheat the oven to 190°C (375°F, Gas Mark 5).

2. In an electric mixer, beat butter and sugar together until light and fluffy.

3. Stir in flour to create a smooth paste. Turn onto a work surface and gently roll out until the paste is 1cm (½ in) thick.

4. Cut into desired shape (squares, rounds or fingers) and place onto a baking tray.

5. Sprinkle with caster sugar and chill in the fridge for 20 minutes.

6. Bake in the oven for 20 minutes, or until pale golden-brown. Allow to cool on a wire rack and dust with icing sugar before serving.

CHOC-CHOC HAZELNUT COOKIES

INGREDIENTS

2½ cups (310g, 10oz) plain flour

1 tsp bicarbonate of soda

½ tsp salt

¾ cup (90g, 3oz) cocoa

225g (8oz) butter, room temperature

1 cup (220g, 8oz) sugar

1 cup (155g, 5oz) light brown sugar

2 eggs

1 tsp vanilla extract

1 cup (170g, 6oz) chocolate chips

1 cup (140g, 5oz) chopped hazelnuts

½ tsp sea salt

METHOD

1. Preheat oven to 180°C (350°F, Gas Mark 4). Line a baking tray with greaseproof paper.

2. Sift flour into a medium bowl and add bicarbonate of soda, salt, and cocoa. Set aside.

3. With an electric mixer, cream butter and sugars together on a medium speed until smooth. Add in eggs, one at a time beating for 30 seconds after each addition. Then add vanilla extract and mix until combined.

4. Gradually add flour mixture and beat on low speed until just combined. Stir in the chocolate chips and hazelnuts.

5. Scoop the dough into rounded tablespoons and place on prepared baking tray, about 5cm (2in) apart. Sprinkle each cookie with sea salt.

6. Bake for 10 minutes, or until cookies are firm, but still soft in the centre.

7. Remove from oven and let sit on baking tray for 3 minutes. Move to a wire cooling rack and cool completely.

GINGERBREAD MEN

INGREDIENTS

125g (4oz) butter, room temperature

²/₃ cup (100g, 3oz) brown sugar

¼ cup (60ml, 2fl oz) maple syrup

1 egg, lightly beaten

2½ cups (310g, 10oz) plain flour

½ tsp bicarbonate of soda

1 tbsp ground ginger

2 tsps ground cinnamon

2 cups (340g, 12oz) white chocolate melts

1 cup (170g, 6oz) dark chocolate melts, to decorate

METHOD

1. Preheat oven to 180°C (350°F, Gas Mark 4). Line three baking trays with greaseproof paper.

2. Using an electric mixer, beat butter and sugar until light and fluffy. Add maple syrup and egg and beat to combine.

3. Sift flour, bicarbonate of soda, ginger and cinnamon over butter mixture. Stir until just combined and a soft dough forms.

4. Place dough on a floured surface and knead gently until smooth. Shape the dough into a disc and wrap in plastic wrap. Refrigerate for 1 hour.

5. Roll dough out to a thickness of 5mm (¼in). Cut shapes from dough using a gingerbread man cutter. Place on baking trays about 2cm (1in) apart.

6. Bake one tray at a time for 20 minutes, or until firm to touch. Stand on trays for 5 minutes, before transferring to a wire rack to cool completely.

7. Place white and dark melts in separate small saucepans over a medium heat, stirring every 30 seconds until smooth. Spoon into a small piping bag. Pipe faces and decoration onto gingerbread men. Allow 10 minutes for chocolate to set before serving.

PEANUT BUTTER COOKIES

INGREDIENTS

230g (8oz) butter, room temperature

²/₃ cup (230g, 8oz) smooth peanut butter

1 cup (155g, 5oz) light brown sugar, packed

1½ tsps vanilla essence

2½ cups (310g, 10oz) plain flour

¼ cup (40g, 1½ oz) cornflour

¾ cup (90g, 3oz) peanuts, very finely chopped

METHOD

1. Preheat oven to 180°C (350°F, Gas Mark 4) and line a baking tray with greaseproof paper.

2. Using an electric mixer, beat butter, peanut butter and brown sugar until smooth and creamy. Beat in vanilla.

3. Stir in flour and cornflour until mixture holds together. Add in the chopped peanuts and stir until combined.

4. Roll out on floured surface to about 5mm (¼in) thickness and cut with cookie cutters or shape into small balls and flatten. Use the tines of a fork to mark the cookies. Place cookies on baking tray leaving a space between each.

5. Bake for 25 minutes, or until cookies are firm and golden brown. Cool on the tray for 5 minutes then remove to a wire rack to cool completely.

CLASSIC ANZAC BISCUITS

INGREDIENTS

1 cup (90g, 3oz) rolled oats

1 cup (125g, 4oz) plain flour, sifted

1 cup (155g, 5oz) firmly packed brown sugar

½ cup (40g, 1½ oz) desiccated coconut

125g (4oz) butter, chopped

2 tbsps golden syrup

1½ tbsps water

½ tsp bicarbonate of soda

METHOD

1. Preheat oven to 160°C (325°F, Gas Mark 3). Grease and line a baking tray with greaseproof paper.

2. Combine oats, flour, sugar and coconut in a large bowl. Set aside.

3. Place butter, golden syrup and water in a small saucepan over low heat. Stir until smooth. Add bicarb and dry ingredients and stir to combine well.

4. Measure level tablespoons of mixture and roll into balls. Flatten slightly and then place evenly spaced on tray. Bake for 20 minutes or until golden. Cool on tray and then move to a wire rack.

Note: Anzac biscuits should be soft to touch. They will crispen on cooling. Increase/decrease the oven temperature and/or the baking time to produce crispier/softer biscuits.

BLUEBERRY CRUMBLE CHEESECAKE BARS

INGREDIENTS

Base

10 shortbread biscuits, finely crushed

3 tbsps sugar

4 tbsps butter, melted

Pinch of salt

Blueberry filling

1 cup (100g, 3½ oz) blueberries

2 tsps sugar

2 tsps plain flour

1 tbsp lemon juice

Crumble

1 cup (125g, 4oz) plain flour

¼ cup (40g, 1½ oz) brown sugar

¼ cup (55g, 2oz) sugar

7 tbsps butter, cold

Cheesecake

340g (12oz) cream cheese

½ cup (125ml, 4fl oz) sour cream

½ cup (110g, 4oz) sugar

1½ tsp vanilla essence

2 eggs

METHOD

1. Preheat oven to 160°C (325°F, Gas Mark 3). Line a deep 20cm (8in) square baking tin with greaseproof paper. Remove cream cheese, sour cream and eggs from fridge to bring to room temperature.

2. In a medium-sized mixing bowl combine ingredients for base, then spread evenly into prepared tin. Place in oven and bake for 10 minutes. Set aside to cool.

3. Meanwhile, rinse blueberries and pat dry with a kitchen towel. In a small bowl, combine blueberries, sugar, flour and lemon juice. Mix to combine and set aside.

4. In a medium-sized mixing bowl, combine all ingredients for crumble topping. Rub with fingertips until a coarse crumb forms.

5. In the bowl of an electric mixer, beat cream cheese, sour cream and sugar until smooth. Add vanilla and one egg. Mix until combined, then add the remaining egg, again mixing until combined.

6. Pour cheesecake mixture over crust and smooth over with a spatula. Spoon blueberry mixture over cheesecake and then top with crumble.

7. Place in oven and bake for 45 minutes or until the crumble is golden brown in color. Remove and allow to cool to room temperature before transferring to fridge to chill for at least 4 hours before serving. Cut into bars to serve.

FLORENTINES

INGREDIENTS

¼ cup (45g, 2oz) mixed dried fruit, cherries or candied orange peel

1¾ cups (70g, 2½ oz) sugar

25g (1oz) butter

2 tsps plain flour

¼ cup (60ml, 2fl oz) crème fraîche

50g (2oz) flaked almonds

(30g, 1oz) mixed seeds (sunflower, sesame, poppy seeds)

150g (5½ oz) dark or milk chocolate

METHOD

1. Preheat the oven to 180°C (350°F, Gas Mark 4) and line two baking trays with greaseproof paper.

2. Finely chop the dried fruit or peel.

3. Place a small saucepan over a low heat and add the sugar, butter and flour, stirring to combine. Keep stirring until the sugar has dissolved, then gradually add the crème fraîche.

4. Take off the heat and stir in the flaked almonds, seeds and dried fruit or peel.

5. Drop small mounds of mixture onto the baking trays, leaving a gap between each to allow room to spread. Press down slightly.

6. Bake for 15 minutes, until golden. Leave to cool a little on the tray before cooling on a rack.

7. Meanwhile, melt chocolate in a heatproof bowl over a saucepan of simmering water, then, using a spoon, sweep it back and forth over the florentines.

CRANBERRY AND CHOCOLATE COOKIES

INGREDIENTS

1 cup (125g, 4oz) plain flour, sifted

¾ tsp ground cinnamon

½ tsp baking powder

½ tsp bicarbonate of soda

½ tsp salt

110g (4oz) butter, room temperature

½ cup (80g, 3oz) light brown sugar

½ cup (110g, 4oz) sugar

1 egg

½ tsp pure vanilla extract

3½ cups (310g, 11oz) oats

1 cup (160g, 6oz) dried cranberries

125g (4oz) dark chocolate, chopped

METHOD

1. Preheat oven to 180°C (350°F, Gas Mark 4). Line two baking trays with greaseproof paper.

2. In a medium bowl, combine flour, cinnamon, baking powder, bicarbonate of soda and salt.

3. In an electric mixer, beat the butter and sugars together until light and fluffy. Add egg and vanilla and beat until smooth. With the machine on low speed, gradually add the flour mixture. Add oats, cranberries and chocolate chunks. Mix until incorporated and a stiff dough forms.

4. Scoop mounds of the dough into balls. Arrange evenly spaced on each baking tray. Press slightly to flatten and then bake for 15 minutes until golden on the edges. Allow the cookies to cool on the baking tray for 20 minutes before serving.

WHITE CHOCOLATE MACADAMIA BISCUITS

INGREDIENTS

250g (9oz) butter,
room temperature

1 cup (155g, 5oz) firmly
packed brown sugar

½ cup (110g, 4oz) sugar

2 tsps vanilla extract

2 eggs

2½ cups (310g, 10oz) plain
flour, sifted

1 tsp baking powder

¾ cup (90g, 3oz)
macadamia nuts, chopped

180g (6oz) white chocolate,
chopped (or chocolate
chips)

METHOD

1. Preheat oven to 180°C (350°F, Gas Mark 4) and line three baking
   trays with greaseproof paper.

2. Using an electric mixer, cream butter, sugars and vanilla until
   light and fluffy. Add eggs, 1 at a time, beating well after each
   addition.

3. Add flour, baking powder, nuts and chocolate. Stir with a large
   metal spoon until well combined.

4. Drop spoonfuls of mixture onto baking trays and flatten slightly.

5. Bake each tray separately in the centre of the oven for 15
   minutes or until golden and firm to the touch.

6. Remove from oven and stand on trays for 5 minutes. Transfer to
   a wire rack to cool completely.

SERVES 15 ★ PREP 35MIN ★ COOK TIME 10MIN

RED VELVET WHOOPIE PIES

INGREDIENTS

Whoopie pies

125g (4oz) butter, room temperature

1¼ cup (195g, 6½ oz) brown sugar

2 eggs

½ tsp vanilla extract

2 cups (250g, 8oz) plain flour

½ tsp baking soda

¼ tsp salt

2 tbsps cocoa powder

½ cup (125ml, 4fl oz) buttermilk

2 tbsps red food colouring

Cream cheese frosting

75g (3oz) butter, room temperature

200g (7oz) cream cheese, room temperature

1½ cups (235g, 8oz) icing sugar mixture, sifted

1 tsp vanilla extract

METHOD

1. Preheat oven to 190°C (375°F, Gas Mark 5). Line two baking trays with greaseproof paper.

2. Using an electric mixer, combine butter and sugar in a large mixing bowl and cream until light and fluffy. Add one egg and vanilla extract and beat to combine. Add remaining egg and beat for 1 minute.

3. In a separate bowl sift together flour, baking soda, salt and cocoa powder.

4. Add half the dry ingredients to the cream mixture, then add half the buttermilk, and then beat until just combined. Repeat with the remaining dry ingredients and buttermilk. Add the food colouring and stir to combine.

5. Using an ice-cream scoop, drop batter onto the prepared baking trays. Score crosses on the top of the batter using the tines of a fork.

6. Place in the oven and bake for 10 minutes or until tops spring back to the touch. Remove from the oven and allow to cool completely.

7. Meanwhile, using an electric mixer beat butter, cream cheese, icing sugar and vanilla extract until smooth.

8. To assemble each pie, pipe frosting on the flat side of one cookie and then sandwich with another cookie.

CHOCOLATE CHIP COOKIES

INGREDIENTS

150g (5½ oz) butter, room temperature

½ cup (100g, 3½ oz) caster sugar

½ cup (80g, 3oz) packed brown sugar

1 tsp vanilla extract

1 egg

1¾ cups (215g, 7oz) plain flour

½ cup (85g, 3oz) dark chocolate chips

½ cup (85g, 3oz) milk chocolate chips

METHOD

1. Preheat oven to 180°C (350°F, Gas Mark 4) and line two baking trays with greaseproof paper.

2. Place butter, sugars and vanilla in an electric mixer and beat for 1-2 minutes until smooth and well combined. Add egg and whisk until combined.

3. Add the flour in two batches, stirring after each addition. Add the dark and milk choc chips and mix thoroughly.

4. Measure level tablespoons of the dough. Roll into balls and place evenly spaced on prepared trays. Press down slightly on each ball.

5. Bake for 15 minutes or until golden. When cooked, remove from the oven and transfer to a wire rack to cool.

6. Store in an airtight container for up to 1 week.

DOUBLE CHOC CHIP COOKIES

INGREDIENTS

125g (4oz) butter,
room temperature

½ cup (100g, 3½ oz)
caster sugar

½ cup (80g, 3oz)
brown sugar

1 egg

1 tsp vanilla extract

1½ cups (185g, 6oz)
self-raising flour

½ cup (60g, 2oz) cocoa

¾ cup (130g, 4oz) dark
chocolate chips

METHOD

1. Preheat oven to 160°C (320°F, Gas Mark 3) and line two baking trays with greaseproof paper.

2. In an electric mixer, cream together butter and sugars until light and fluffy. Add egg and vanilla and whisk until combined.

3. Stir in flour and cocoa then fold through chocolate chips.

4. Measure level tablespoons, rolling into balls and placing on prepared trays approximately 3cm (1in) apart. Press down slightly on each ball.

5. Bake for 15 minutes or until golden brown. When cooked, remove from the oven and transfer to a wire rack to cool.

6. Store in an airtight container for up to 1 week.

CHOCOLATE ALMOND BISCOTTI

INGREDIENTS

2 cups (250g, 8oz) plain flour

1 cup (220g, 8oz) sugar

⅓ cup (35g, 1oz) cocoa powder

1 tsp bicarbonate of soda

¼ tsp salt

2 eggs

2 egg whites

¾ tsp vanilla extract

⅓ cup (45g, 1½ oz) whole almonds, toasted

⅓ cup (55g, 2oz) chocolate chips

I egg, beaten, for wash

Flour, for dusting

METHOD

1. Preheat the oven to 180°C (350°F, Gas Mark 4) and prepare a baking tray with greaseproof paper.

2. Combine flour, sugar, cocoa powder, bicarbonate of soda and salt in a large bowl.

2. In the bowl of an electric mixer, beat eggs, egg whites and vanilla extract on a medium speed. Reduce speed to low and gradually add the flour mixture. Mix almonds and chocolate chips together then add to mixture and blend just until combined.

4. Transfer to a floured surface and roll dough into 2 logs 5cm (2in) wide. Place logs on prepared baking tray and brush with beaten egg.

5. Bake for 30 minutes or until golden brown. Cool then cut diagonally into slices 1cm (½in) thick.

6. Place slices on a freshly-lined tray and bake for 10 minutes until toasted. Cool. Store in an airtight container.

SERVES 12 ★ PREP 30MIN ★ COOK TIME 30MIN

CHOCOLATE CHEESECAKE BROWNIE

INGREDIENTS

150g (5oz) butter, chopped

300g (10oz) dark cooking chocolate, chopped

3 eggs

1 cup (220g, 8oz) caster sugar

1 tsp vanilla essence

1¾ cups (215g, 7oz) plain flour

¼ cup (60ml, 2fl oz) sour cream

250g (9oz) cream cheese, room temperature

METHOD

1. Preheat oven to 180°C (350°F, Gas Mark 4) and line a 20cm (8in) cake tin with greaseproof paper, allowing some overhang.

2. Combine butter and chocolate in a saucepan over low heat. Cook, stirring constantly, for 5 minutes or until chocolate just melts and mixture is smooth. Remove from heat and set aside to cool.

3. Add two beaten eggs, ⅔ cup (140g, 5oz) sugar and vanilla essence to the chocolate mixture, and stir to combine. Add flour and sour cream and stir until well combined.

4. Using an electric beater mix the cream cheese and remaining sugar in a bowl until smooth. Add the remaining egg and beat until combined.

5. Spoon chocolate and cream cheese alternately over base of tin. Place in oven and bake for 30 minutes or until a skewer inserted into the centre comes out clean.

6. Remove from oven and set aside in the tin to cool for at least 30 minutes. Cut into small squares to serve.

JAM DROPS

INGREDIENTS

125g (4oz) butter,
room temperature

¾ cup (165g, 6oz)
caster sugar

2 eggs

2 cups (250g, 8oz)
self-raising flour, sifted

Pinch of salt

¼ cup (90g, 3oz)
strawberry jam

METHOD

1. Preheat oven to 180°C (350°F, Gas Mark 4)and line two baking trays with greaseproof paper.

2. In an electric mixer, cream butter and sugar together until light and fluffy. Next add the eggs and beat until combined. Add flour and salt, mixing to form a dough.

3. Measure a teaspoon of mixture and roll into a ball. Place on baking tray. Repeat until all mixture has been used up, leaving a gap between each to allow room to spread.

4. Press a finger into the centre of each ball to create a hole. Fill each hole with the strawberry jam.

5. Bake for 20 minutes. Remove from oven and leave to cool on tray for 2-3 minutes before moving to a wire rack to cool fully.

SERVES 30 ★ PREP 30MIN ★ COOK TIME 45MIN

CANTUCCI

INGREDIENTS

2 cups (250g, 8oz) flour, sifted

¾ cup (165g, 6oz) sugar

1 tsp baking powder

2 eggs

1 tbsp honey

1 tsp orange zest

1 tsp amaretto or ½ tsp almond extract

125g (4oz) almonds

Flour, for dusting

METHOD

1. Preheat the oven to 180°C (350°F, Gas Mark 4) and line a baking tray with greaseproof paper.

2. In a large bowl, combine the dry ingredients. Next add the eggs, honey, orange zest and amaretto and mix all the ingredients together well. When the mixture is soft and crumbly, fold in the almonds.

3. Transfer the dough onto a floured surface and roll it into two logs 5cm (2in) wide. Place the logs on the baking tray.

4. Bake for 30 minutes, until golden brown. Remove logs from the oven and cool for about 10 minutes. Slice diagonally into slices.

5. Put the slices back on a freshly-lined tray and bake for 15 minutes until toasted.

6. Remove the cantucci from the oven and cool on a wire rack. Store in an airtight container.

MUESLI BARS

INGREDIENTS

1 cup (90g, 3oz) oats

1 cup (90g, 3oz) desiccated coconut

½ cup (40g, 1½ oz) flax seeds

½ cup (40g, 1½ oz) sesame seeds

½ cup (40g, 1½ oz) sunflower seeds

½ cup (60g, 2oz) cashews

½ cup (80g, 3oz) sultanas

½ cup (80g, 3oz) cranberries

125g (4oz) butter

½ cup (180g, 6oz) honey

⅓ cup (50g, 2oz) brown sugar

METHOD

1. Line a 3cm (1in)-deep 28 x 16cm (11 x 6in) baking tin with greaseproof paper.

2. Place oats, coconut, flax seeds, sesame seeds, sunflower kernels and cashew nuts in a frying pan over a medium heat and stir for 10 minutes or until golden and lightly toasted. Place in a large bowl to cool and stir in sultanas and cranberries. Set aside.

3. Place butter, honey and sugar in a saucepan over a medium heat and cook, stirring constantly, for 5 minutes or until sugar has dissolved. Reduce heat to low and simmer without stirring for 5 minutes.

4. Add wet mixture to dry ingredients and mix thoroughly to combine.

5. Spoon mixture into the tin and press down firmly. Transfer to the fridge and allow to set for 2 hours. Remove and cut into rectangular slices.

SERVES 10 ★ PREP 20MIN ★ COOK TIME 5MIN (PLUS CHILLING)
EASY CHOCOLATE NUT SLICE

INGREDIENTS

1 pkt plain sweet biscuits

55g (2oz) vegetable shortening

½ cup (125ml, 4fl oz) coconut cream

1 x 400g (14oz) can condensed milk

½ cup (60g, 2oz) cocoa

1 cup (125g, 4oz) crushed peanuts

1 cup (90g, 3oz) shredded coconut

Finely grated milk chocolate, to finish

METHOD

1. Place the biscuits in the bowl of a food processor and pulse until rough breadcrumbs form.

2. Melt the shortening in a large saucepan over a medium heat. Remove from heat. Add coconut cream and condensed milk and stir briskly until combined. Stir in the cocoa, crushed nuts and coconut.

3. Press into a 13 x 27cm (5 x 10½ in) slice tin and refrigerate for 30 minutes or until firm.

4 Sprinkle grated chocolate over the top and cut into squares to serve.

CHOCOLATE CARAMEL SLICE

INGREDIENTS

Base

1 cup (125g, 4oz) plain flour, sifted

½ cup (80g, 3oz) brown sugar

½ cup (40g, 1½ oz) desiccated coconut

125g (4oz) butter, melted

1 tsp vanilla essence

Filling

1 x 400g (14oz) can sweetened condensed milk

2 tbsps golden syrup

60g (2oz) butter, melted

Topping

60g (2oz) vegetable shortening, chopped

125g (4oz) cooking chocolate, chopped

METHOD

1. Preheat oven to 180°C (350°F, Gas Mark 4). Line a 28 x 18cm (11 x 7in) deep-sided baking tray with greaseproof paper, cutting corners to fit.

2. Combine base ingredients in a bowl. Mix well. Press into prepared tin. Place in the oven and bake for 15 minutes, or until lightly golden. Remove from oven and set aside to cool.

3. In a saucepan over medium heat, combine filling ingredients and cook, stirring constantly, for 8-10 minutes or until the caramel sauce is thick and golden. Pour caramel over base. Place in the oven and bake for 12 minutes or until firm. Remove from oven and allow to cool completely. Refrigerate for 3 hours, or until completely set.

4. Put shortening and chocolate into a heatproof bowl over a saucepan of simmering water. Stir until just melted. Pour chocolate over caramel. Refrigerate for 1 hour or until set. Cut into squares to serve.

STRAWBERRY MACARONS

INGREDIENTS

Shells

1¾ cups (210g, 8oz) almond meal

1½ cups (210g, 8oz) icing sugar

3 egg whites (170g (6oz) egg whites)

2 drops rose food colouring

1½ cups (235g, 8oz) sugar

⅔ cup (160ml, 5fl oz) water

Filling

250g (9oz) butter, room temperature

2 cups (310g, 10oz) icing sugar

Pinch of salt

1 tsp vanilla extract

¼ cup (90g, 3oz) pureed strawberries

METHOD

1. Preheat the oven to 180°C (350°F, Gas Mark 4) and line three baking trays with greaseproof paper.

2. In a medium bowl, blend together the almond meal, icing sugar and 2 tablespoons of egg white and blend to form a paste.

3. In an electric mixer, whisk the egg white and food colouring until foamy. Keep the machine running on a very low speed for the next step.

4. In a saucepan over a medium-high heat, stir together sugar and water. Using a thermometer heat the mixture to 120°C (250°F) and then immediately remove from the heat and pour down the side of the mixing bowl into the beaten egg whites. Increase the speed to high and beat until a thick meringue has formed.

5. Gently fold meringue into the almond meal mixture in three batches. Transfer to a piping bag and pipe rounds about 5cm (2in) apart. Repeat until batter has all been used.

6. Place in the oven and bake for 10 minutes until tops have hardened. Allow to cool for 5 minutes before transferring to a wire rack.

7. Use an electric mixer to cream butter until light and fluffy. Add icing sugar and salt and mix until the sugar is fully incorporated and the mixture is creamy and fluffy, about 6 minutes.

8. Add the vanilla and strawberry puree and whisk for 3 minutes until creamy.

9. To assemble, match the shells together in pairs. Pipe a small round of buttercream on the flat side of the macaron shell. Top with the other matching macaron shell.

PUMPKIN AND WALNUT SLICE

INGREDIENTS

Cake

2 cups (250g, 8oz) flour

1 tsp bicarbonate of soda

¾ tsp salt

1 tsp cinnamon

½ tsp ground ginger

¼ tsp ground nutmeg

¼ tsp ground cloves

250g (9oz) butter, melted

¾ cup (165g, 6oz) sugar

½ cup (80g, 3oz) brown sugar

1 egg

2 tsps vanilla exract

1 cup (225g, 8oz) cooked pumpkin, mashed

1 cup (125g, 4oz) walnuts, chopped

Topping

1 tbsp plain flour

5 tbsps sugar

½ tsp ground cinnamon

1 tbsp butter, room temperature

METHOD

1. Preheat oven to 180°C (350°F, Gas Mark 4) and line a 23cm (9in) cake tin with greaseproof paper.

2. In a large mixing bowl combine flour, bicarb, salt and spices. Set aside.

3. In a large mixing bowl whisk the melted butter and sugars. Add the egg, vanilla and pumpkin and mix well.

4. Add dry ingredients into wet ingredients, then add the walnuts and blend together with a spatula or metal spoon until fully incorporated.

5. Scrape batter into tin and bake for 30 minutes or until a skewer inserted in the centre comes out clean.

6. Remove from oven and cool for 5 minutes in tin before transferring to a wire rack to cool completely.

7. In a small bowl, blend the topping ingredients with your fingertips until crumbled. Sprinkle crumb onto cake. Slice.

SERVES 12 ★ PREP 25MIN ★ COOK TIME 30MIN

EASY BEETROOT BROWNIE

INGREDIENTS

250g (9oz) dark chocolate, chopped

250g (9oz) butter, cut into cubes

1½ cups (250g, 9oz) beetroot, cooked

3 eggs

1 tsp vanilla essence

1 cup (220g, 8oz) caster sugar

¼ cup (30g, 1oz) cocoa powder

½ cup (60g, 2oz) rice flour (or plain flour)

1 tsp baking powder

1 cup (100g, 3½ oz) almond meal

METHOD

1. Preheat oven to 180°C (350°F, Gas Mark 4). Line a rectangular tin with greaseproof paper.

2. Melt chocolate and butter in a heatproof bowl placed over a pan of simmering water.

3. Place cooked beetroot in a food processor and pulse until pureed. Add the eggs one at a time, followed by the vanilla and sugar, and mix until smooth.

4. Sift cocoa powder, rice flour and baking powder into a bowl and stir in almond meal. Stir beetroot mixture into the melted chocolate and then fold in the dry ingredients.

5. Pour the mixture into the tin and bake in the oven for 30 minutes, until just firm to the touch and a skewer inserted in the centre comes out slightly sticky. Leave to cool in the tin and then cut into squares.

CREAM CHEESE AND DARK CHOCOLATE BARS

INGREDIENTS

Cake

1 cup (155g, 5oz) packed brown sugar

55g (2oz) butter, melted

1 egg, beaten

½ tsp vanilla extract

4 cups (500g, 1lb) plain flour

¼ tsp baking powder

½ tsp salt

Ganache

220g (8oz) dark chocolate, chopped

1 cup (250ml, 8fl oz) thickened cream

1 tbsp butter, room temperature

Cream cheese

455g (1lb) cream cheese, room temperature

1 cup (220g, 8oz) sugar

2 eggs

½ tsp vanilla extract

Fresh mint, to garnish

METHOD

1. Preheat oven to 180°C (350°F, Gas Mark 4) and grease a baking dish.

2. Combine brown sugar, butter, eggs and vanilla in a large bowl, and stir until smooth.

3. In separate bowl, combine flour, baking powder and salt, then gradually mix into wet ingredients until just combined. Don't over-mix.

4. Pour mixture into baking dish and bake for 20 minutes, or until golden brown. Remove from oven to cool.

5. Meanwhile, place chocolate in a medium, heatproof bowl. Place cream in small saucepan over medium heat and bring to a simmer, then pour cream over chocolate pieces. Stand for 5 minutes, or until chocolate has softened.

6. Add butter and stir until smooth. Set aside to cool slightly (but still be pourable).

7. Beat cream cheese, sugar, eggs and vanilla extract together in a medium bowl or mixer on medium speed, until smooth.

8. Spread half of the ganache over cooled cake layer and then add cream cheese mixture over top. Spread into an even layer using a spatula.

9. Drizzle remaining ganache over top and refrigerate for a minimum of 30 minutes before slicing into bars and serving. Garnish with fresh mint, if desired.

LEMON BLUEBERRY MADELEINES

INGREDIENTS

2 eggs

½ cup (110g, 4oz) sugar

1 tsp vanilla extract

½ lemon, zested

1 cup (125g, 4oz) plain flour

¼ tsp salt

¼ tsp baking powder

125g (4oz) butter, melted

1 cup (100g, 3½ oz) fresh blueberries

Icing sugar, to finish

METHOD

1. Preheat the oven to 180°C (350°F, Gas Mark 4) and lightly grease two 12-hole madeleine pans. Set aside.

2. Using an electric mixer on a high speed, cream eggs and sugar for 3-4 minutes until light and fluffy.

3. Add vanilla, lemon zest, flour, salt and baking powder. Reduce mixer to a low speed and slowly pour in the melted butter. Mix until well incorporated but not over-worked.

4. Divide batter evenly in the pans, and press a few blueberries into each one.

5. Place in the oven and bake for about 10 minutes or until golden and darkening around the edges.

6. Remove from the oven and cool for 5 minutes, then invert onto a wire rack to cool completely. Sift icing sugar over the top of the madeleines before serving.

CHOC CORNFLAKE CRUNCHIES

INGREDIENTS

455g (1lb) milk chocolate

4 cups (110g, 4oz) cornflakes

METHOD

1. Place chocolate in a bowl in the microwave. Cook on high in bursts of 30 seconds until melted. The chocolate should be warm but not hot to the touch.

2. Put cornflakes into a large mixing bowl, and pour over half of the melted chocolate. Use a rubber spatula or wooden spoon to mix until the cornflakes are coated evenly with chocolate. The tempered chocolate will begin to set quickly. When set, repeat with the remaining melted chocolate to give a second coat.

3. Quickly scoop the chocolate cornflakes into small mounds onto baking trays lined with greaseproof paper to prevent the cookies from sticking.

4. Place the baking trays in the fridge for 5 minutes (but no more than 10 minutes) to allow the chocolate to harden.

5. Store in an airtight container in a cool, dry area for up to two weeks.

MANGO CREAM CHEESE SLICE

INGREDIENTS

2 cups (180g, 6oz) oats

1 cup (125g, 4oz) flour

²/₃ cup (100g, 3oz) packed brown sugar

¾ cup (165g, 6oz) sugar

170g (6oz) butter

455g (1lb) cream cheese

2 eggs

1 tsp vanilla essence

1 mango, peeled and mashed

½ tsp almond extract

1 tsp cinnamon

¼ tsp nutmeg

2 tbsps sugar

METHOD

1. Preheat oven to 180°C (350°F, Gas Mark 4). and line a 23 x 33cm (9 x 13in) baking tin with greaseproof paper.

2. Combine oats, flour, brown sugar and ¼ cup (55g, 2oz) of sugar in a large bowl. Add butter and rub with fingertips until crumbly. Set aside 1 cup of the crumble and press remainder into base of tin.

3. Place in the oven and bake for 10 minutes. Remove and set aside to cool slightly.

4. In a mixing bowl, combine cream cheese, eggs, ½ cup (110g, 4oz) of sugar and vanilla. Mix until smooth and spread evenly over oat crust.

5. Place mango and almond extract in a bowl and stir, then spread over the cream cheese mixture. Sprinkle over reserved crumble and top with spices and sugar.

6. Return to oven and bake for 25 minutes or until golden. Cool completely and cut into bars.

LEMON BARS

INGREDIENTS

Crust

2 cups (250g, 8oz)
plain flour

½ cup (110g, 4oz) sugar

¼ tsp salt

250g (9oz) salted butter,
cubed

Filling

1 cup (220g, 8oz)
caster sugar

¼ cup (30g, 1oz) plain flour

4 eggs

4 lemons, juiced and zested

Icing sugar, for dusting

Fresh mint, to garnish
(optional)

METHOD

1. Preheat oven to 180°C (350°F, Gas Mark 4) and line a 28 x 18cm (11 x 7in) deep-sided baking tin with greaseproof paper, cutting corners to fit.

2. Stir together flour, sugar, and salt. Add butter to the bowl and rub together with fingertips until the mixture resembles loose crumbs. Press into the prepared tin and bake for 20 minutes or until golden around the edges.

3. Mix caster sugar and flour together in a large bowl. Add the eggs and whisk to combine. Add the lemon zest and juice and whisk further until fully combined. Pour over the crust and bake for 20 minutes.

4. Allow to cool in the fridge for 2 hours or more until set, then sift icing sugar over the top before cutting into squares.

HOMEMADE OREO COOKIES

INGREDIENTS

Cookies

1¼ cup (155g, 5oz) plain flour

½ cup (60g, 2oz) cocoa powder

1 tsp baking soda

¼ tsp salt

110g (4oz) butter, room temperature

¾ cup (165g, 6oz) sugar

¼ cup (40g, 1½ oz) packed brown sugar

1 egg

1 tsp vanilla extract

½ cup (80g, 3oz) milk chocolate chips

Cream filling

60g (2oz) butter, room temperature

60g (2oz) vegetable shortening

2 cups (310g, 10oz) icing sugar

2 tsps vanilla extract

METHOD

1. Sift flour, cocoa powder, baking soda and salt over a large bowl. Set aside.

2. Using an electric mixer, cream butter and sugar on medium speed for 1 minute until pale. Add brown sugar and beat until light and fluffy. Add egg and vanilla extract, and beat until combined. Mix dry ingredients into wet ingredients using a wooden spoon. With the mixer on a low setting, slowly beat until a dough forms. Cover and chill in the refrigerator for 30 minutes.

3. Preheat oven to 180°C (350°F, Gas Mark 4) and line two large baking trays with greaseproof paper. Remove the dough from the refrigerator.

4. Place 10 balls of dough on each baking tray. Add a sprinkle of chocolate chips onto the top of each and press down to flatten.

5. Place one baking tray in the oven and bake for 8 minutes or until soft and springy to touch. Repeat with the other batch. Remove from the oven and allow to cool 5 minutes before transferring to a wire rack to cool completely.

6. Meanwhile, using an electric mixer, beat butter and shortening together on high speed for 1 minute or until creamy. Add the icing sugar and vanilla. Beat on low to combine and then switch to high and beat for 1 more minute until creamy.

7. Spread filling on the flat side of one cookie and sandwich with another cookie. Repeat with the remaining cookies.

NUT BARS

INGREDIENTS

1 cup (350g, 12oz) honey

1 tbsp butter

½ tsp vanilla

¼ tsp salt

1 cup (140g, 5oz) dry roasted, unsalted nuts

METHOD

1. Preheat oven to 160°C (320°F, Gas Mark 3). Prepare two large sheets of greaseproof paper.

2. Place honey, butter, vanilla, and salt in a saucepan over a high heat and bring to the boil, stirring constantly. Reduce heat and simmer undisturbed for at least 10 minutes until the caramel turns dark brown.

3. Cool the liquid for 2 minutes and then add nuts. Stir until nuts are well coated.

4. On a flat surface, place down a sheet of greaseproof paper. Scrape over the nut mixture and place the other piece of greaseproof paper on top. Use hands or a rolling pin to spread the nuts out evenly. Remove top sheet of greaseproof paper.

5. Place in the oven for 1 hour. Remove from oven and leave to cool.

   Note: Store in the refrigerator and eat cold.

DATE AND WALNUT SLICE

INGREDIENTS

½ cup (80g, 3oz) chopped walnuts

1 cup (90g, 3oz) coconut

1 cup (155g, 5oz) packed brown sugar

1 cup (140g, 5oz) dates, chopped

1 cup (90g, 3oz) oats

125g (5oz) butter

1 tbsp golden syrup

1 egg, beaten

Handful of walnuts, halved, to decorate

METHOD

1. Preheat oven to 180°C (350°F, Gas Mark 4) and line a 18 x 28cm (7 x 11in) slice tin.

2. In a large mixing bowl, combine dry ingredients, breaking up any lumps with the back of a spoon.

3. Melt butter in a small saucepan over low heat. When melted, add golden syrup and stir well.

4. Pour syrup over dry ingredients. Add egg and stir until mixture is well combined. Press mixture into slice pan.

5. Place in the oven and bake 30 minutes. Remove and cool in the tin.

6. To serve, decorate with walnut halves and slice into squares.

FUDGY BROWNIES

INGREDIENTS

300g (10oz) dark chocolate, cut into pieces

3 tbsps cocoa powder

280g (8oz) butter

1 cup (220g, 8oz) sugar

1 cup (155g, 5oz) brown sugar, packed

1 tbsp vanilla extract

1 tsp salt

1 tsp instant coffee

4 eggs

1 cup (125g, 4oz) plain flour

½ cup (80g, 3oz) dark chocolate chips

½ cup (80g, 3oz) milk chocolate chips

METHOD

1. Preheat oven to 180°C (350°F, Gas Mark 4) and line a 23cm (9in) square tin with greaseproof paper.

2. In a heatproof bowl, combine dark chocolate, cocoa powder and butter. Set the bowl over a small saucepan of simmering water and melt, stirring occasionally until a smooth ganache comes together. Set aside ½ cup (125ml, 4fl oz) ganache to decorate brownies at the end.

3. Meanwhile, in a large mixing bowl, mix the sugars, vanilla extract, salt, coffee and eggs until well incorporated.

4. Stir melted chocolate mixture into the bowl until smooth. Gently fold in the flour until a batter comes together. Stir in dark and milk chocolate chips.

4. Pour the batter into the prepared tin and bake for 35 minutes, until just set. Remove from oven and allow to cool completely, then remove from the tin.

6. To serve, cut into 16 squares, and drizzle with the reserved chocolate ganache.

CHOC-O-NUT MACARONS

INGREDIENTS

Shells

1 cup (125g, 4oz) toasted hazelnuts

1½ cups (210g, 8oz) icing sugar

10g (¼ oz) cocoa powder

5 egg whites

⅓ cup (70g, 2½ oz) caster sugar

Filling

¼ cup (40g, 1½ oz) chocolate chips

¼ cup (60ml, 2fl oz) thickened cream

100g (3½ oz) chocolate hazelnut spread

Chopped hazelnuts, to decorate

METHOD

1. Preheat the oven to 150°C (300°F, Gas Mark 2). Line two baking trays with greaseproof paper.

2. Pulse hazelnuts and icing sugar in food processor until finely ground.

3. Sift the cocoa powder into the hazelnuts/icing sugar mix. Set aside.

4. Using an electric mixer, beat the egg whites to form stiff, dry peaks. Add sugar and beat until soft and glossy.

5. Add the hazelnut mixture to the egg whites and fold with a rubber spatula to combine until the batter falls from the spatula in ribbons.

6. Spoon the mixture into a large piping bag and pipe in circles on baking trays.

7. Rest for 10 minutes then sprinkle a few drops of water onto the dough, to help retain crispness during baking.

8. Bake for 20 minutes, until the shells are firm when tapped and peel away from paper easily.

9. Cool on baking tray for 10 minutes before removing shells and leaving to cool on a wire rack.

10. Place chocolate chips in a bowl. Heat the cream in a small saucepan until it starts to bubble at the edge. Pour hot cream over the chocolate and leave to stand for 1 minute. Stir until the chocolate is melted. Stir in the chocolate spread until smooth. Leave to cool.

11. To assemble, match up the macarons by size and pipe some ganache onto the flat side of one of the shells then place another shell on top. Repeat until all shells are used. Sprinkle with chopped nuts.

EASY VANILLA SLICE

INGREDIENTS

2 sheets of frozen puff pastry, thawed

2½ cups (625ml, 20fl oz) thickened cream

100g (3½ oz) pkt instant vanilla pudding mix

¼ cup (40g, 1½ oz) icing sugar

½ tsp vanilla extract

Icing sugar, for dusting

METHOD

1. Preheat oven to 220°C (430°F, Gas Mark 7) and line two baking trays with greaseproof paper.

2. Place a pastry sheet onto each tray and prick each sheet with a fork. Score one sheet into squares according to desired serving size.

3. Place in the oven and bake for 10 minutes until pastry is puffed and golden brown. Remove from oven and press down slightly to flatten. Set aside to cool.

4. Using an electric mixer, beat together cream, pudding mixture, icing sugar and vanilla extract for 4 minutes, or until thick and creamy.

5. Pile the cream onto the plain sheet of pastry, smoothing over with a spatula, and top with scored pastry sheet.

6. Dust with extra icing sugar. Serve cut into squares.

SERVES 16 ★ PREP 15MIN ★ COOK TIME 25MIN

PUMPKIN CHOC CHIP BARS

INGREDIENTS

2½ cups (220g, 8oz) rolled oats

½ tsp salt

½ tsp cinnamon

½ tsp ground ginger

½ tsp ground mixed spice

½ cup (80g, 3oz)chocolate chips

¾ cup (170g, 6oz) pumpkin, mashed

2 eggs, beaten

½ cup (125ml, 4fl oz) oil

¼ cup (90g, 3oz) maple syrup

1 tsp vanilla

METHOD

1. Preheat oven to 180°C (350°F, Gas Mark 4) and grease a baking tin.

2. In a large bowl toss oats, salt and spices together until well combined. Stir in chocolate chips.

3. In a separate bowl, combine the mashed pumpkin, eggs, oil, maple syrup and vanilla, and mix until thoroughly combined.

4. Pour mixture into tin and smooth the top with a spatula.

5. Place in oven and bake for 25 minutes or until edges are lightly browned. Cut into squares to serve.

APPLE AND SULTANA SLICE

INGREDIENTS

3 apples, peeled, cored and sliced

½ cup (80g, 3oz) sultanas

½ tsp ground mixed spice

2 cups (250g, 8oz) self-raising flour

1 cup (220g, 8oz) sugar

125g (4oz) butter, cubed

1 egg, beaten

Icing sugar, to finish

METHOD

1. Preheat oven to 190°C (375°F, Gas Mark 5) and line a slice tray with greaseproof paper.

2. Place apples and sultanas and spice in a bowl and mix to combine. Set aside.

3. Combine flour and sugar in a large mixing bowl and stir to combine. Add the butter and rub with fingertips to a fine breadcrumb consistency. Add egg and stir to combine. Bring the dough together with your hands. Turn onto a floured surface and knead to a smooth dough. Cover and transfer to fridge to chill for 10 minutes.

4. Remove dough and separate into two balls. Roll out each to to fit the size of the slice tray.

5. Place a layer of dough on the base of the tray, then pile apple and sultana mix on top. Smooth with a spatula. Place the second layer of pastry over the top and score with a knife to the desired slice sizes.

6. Place in the oven and bake 180°C (350°F, Gas Mark 4) degrees for 25 minutes.

7. Remove from oven and set aside to cool. Sprinkle with icing sugar and cut into squares before serving.

COCONUT ALMOND COOKIES

INGREDIENTS

250g (9oz) butter, room temperature

½ cup (110g, 4oz) sugar

¾ cup (120g, 4oz) packed brown sugar

1 egg, beaten

1 tbsp molasses

1¾ cups (215g, 7oz) plain flour

1 tsp bicarbonate of soda

2 tsp ground ginger

Pinch of salt

2 cups (180g, 6oz) desiccated coconut

2 cups (250g, 8oz) sliced almonds

Desiccated coconut, to decorate

METHOD

1. Preheat oven to 180°C (350°F, Gas Mark 4). Line baking trays with greaseproof paper and set aside.

2. Using an electric mixer on a meduim high speed, cream together butter and sugar until light and fluffy. Add brown sugar and mix until well combined. Add egg and mix until incorporated. Add molasses and stir to combine.

3. In a separate bowl, combine flour, bicarbonate of soda, ground ginger and salt. Add flour mixture to the butter mixture in two batches, stirring to combine after each addition. Add the coconut and almonds in two batches, stirring to combine after each addition.

4. Roll the dough on greaseproof paper to form a log and wrap in plastic wrap. Transfer log to refrigerator to chill for 30 minutes. Remove and unwrap. Slice the cookie dough into rounds, 2cm (1in) thick. Press to flatten dough slightly. Place cookies on baking tray.

5. Transfer baking tray to the oven and bake until golden brown, approximately 15 minutes. Remove from oven and transfer to a wire rack to cool. Cool for 15 minutes before serving. Sprinkle with coconut to serve.

MELTING MOMENTS

INGREDIENTS

Biscuits

125g (4oz) butter,
room temperature

1 cup (125g, 4oz)
plain flour

⅓ cup (50g, 2oz)
icing sugar

⅓ cup (50g, 2oz)
custard powder

Filling

60g (2oz) butter,
room temperature

1 cup (155g, 5oz)
icing sugar

2 tsps finely grated
lemon rind

1 tbsp lemon juice

METHOD

1. Preheat oven to 160°C (325°F, Gas Mark 3). Line two baking trays with greaseproof paper.

2. Using an electric mixer, beat butter until pale and creamy. Add the flour, icing sugar and custard powder and stir to combine with a metal spoon.

3. Roll teaspoonfuls of dough mixture into balls. Place 3cm (1in) apart on the lined trays. Gently flatten with a fork dusted in icing sugar. Depress tines of fork in centre to create marking on the biscuit.

4. Bake for 15 minutes or until just cooked through. Remove and set aside to cool for 30 minutes.

5. Using an electric mixer, beat butter and icing sugar until light and fluffy. Add lemon rind and juice and beat until combined. Spread the butter mixture over the flat side of half the biscuits and sandwich together with remaining biscuits.

GREEK BUTTER COOKIES

INGREDIENTS

8 tbsps icing sugar

⅛ tsp bicarbonate of soda

5 cups (625g, 1lb 4oz) plain flour

Pinch of salt

455g (1lb) butter, room temperature

1 egg

2½ tsps pure almond extract

Icing sugar, for dusting

METHOD

1. Preheat oven to 180°C (350°F, Gas Mark 4) and line two baking trays with greaseproof paper.

2. Sift icing sugar and bicarbonate of soda together in a small bowl. Set aside. Sift flour and salt together in a large bowl. Set aside.

3. Using an electric mixer, beat butter on a medium high speed for 20 minutes. Add egg and almond extract and stir until combined. Add sugar and bicarbonate of soda and beat for a further 10 minutes. With the speed on low, gradually add flour until completely incorporated. If the dough is too sticky, add more flour.

4. Measure 2 tablespoons of dough, roll and shape into a crescent. Repeat with all the mixture. Place on a baking tray and bake for 20 minutes until golden brown.

5. Remove from oven and cool for 10 minutes. Move to a wire rack to cool completely. Dust with icing sugar to finish.

MUFFINS AND SCONES

BANANA, WALNUT AND CHOCOLATE MUFFINS

INGREDIENTS

1¾ cups (215g, 7oz) plain flour

1½ tsps baking powder

¼ tsp bicarbonate of soda

Pinch of salt

2 egg whites

3 medium ripe bananas, mashed

⅔ cup (140g, 5oz) caster sugar

2 tbsps vegetable oil

3 tbsps chocolate chips

3 tbsps chopped walnuts

Chopped walnuts, to decorate

METHOD

1. Preheat oven to 180°C (350°F, Gas Mark 4). Line a 12-hole muffin tray and fill with muffin liners.

2. In large bowl, sift together flour, baking powder, bicarb and salt and mix to combine.

3. In a medium bowl, beat egg whites until just frothy. Add bananas, sugar and oil and mix thoroughly.

4. Stir wet mixture into flour mixture and fold together with a metal spoon until just until combined. Stir in chocolate chips and walnuts. Fill muffin pans with the mixture to about two-thirds full. Press chopped walnuts lightly into the batter to decorate.

5. Place in oven and bake for 20 minutes or until a skewer inserted into the centre comes out clean and tops are lightly browned.

6. Remove from oven and cool slightly in the tin, before transferring out onto a wire rack to cool completely.

CINNAMON ROLLS

INGREDIENTS

Dough

1 cup (250ml, 8fl oz) warm milk

2 eggs

160g (6oz) butter, cubed

6 cups (750g, 1½ lb) plain flour

1¾ tsp salt

½ cup (110g, 4oz) sugar

2½ tsps instant yeast

Filling

160g (6oz) butter, room temperature

1 cup (155g, 5oz) brown sugar, packed

3 tbsps ground cinnamon

Icing

6 tbsps cream cheese, softened

55g (2oz) butter, room temperature

1 cup (155g, 5oz) icing sugar

½ tsp vanilla extract

METHOD

1. Mix together dough ingredients, by hand or in an electric mixer, and knead to make a smooth, soft dough.

2. Place the dough in a lightly oiled bowl, turning to grease all sides. Cover the bowl, and let the dough rise for 1 hour or until nearly doubled in size.

3. Transfer dough to a lightly greased work surface, and roll into a 40 x 55cm (16 x 21in) rectangle. Spread 85g (3oz) butter over the dough using a spatula.

4. Mix brown sugar and cinnamon together, and sprinkle liberally and evenly over the dough.

5. Roll the dough into a log and cut log into 12 slices.

6. Place the rolls in a lightly greased 23 x 33cm (9 x 13in) baking tin. Cover and leave for 30 minutes or until almost double in size.

7. Preheat the oven to 200°C (400°F, Gas Mark 6).

8. Uncover the rolls, and place in the oven to bake for 15 minutes or until golden brown.

9. Meanwhile, beat together cream cheese, butter, icing sugar and vanilla in a small bowl.

10. Remove rolls from the oven and allow to cool until warm. Spread on the icing and serve.

PICNIC MUFFINS

INGREDIENTS

80g (3oz) butter

2 cups (250g, 8oz)
self-raising flour

½ tsp salt

1 egg, lightly beaten

1 cup (250ml, 8fl oz)
milk

100g (3½ oz) feta
cheese, crumbled

100g (3½ oz) sliced ham,
diced

2 tbsps pitted kalamata
olives, chopped

¼ cup (30g, 1oz)
grated cheese

12 small sprigs fresh
rosemary

METHOD

1. Preheat oven to 200°C (390°F, Gas Mark 6). Line a 12-hole muffin tin with paper cases.

2. Melt the butter in a saucepan over a medium heat. Set aside to cool slightly.

3. Sift flour and salt into a large bowl. Make a well in centre.

4. Place melted butter, egg and milk into a jug or small bowl and mix to combine. Pour mixture into well and stir until loosely combined. Fold through feta, ham and olives. Spoon mixture into paper cases filling two-thirds full. Sprinkle with a little grated cheese and insert a rosemary sprig in the top of each muffin.

5. Place in the oven and bake for 20 minutes or until a skewer inserted in the centre comes out clean. Remove and cool in tin for 1 minute. Turn out onto a wire rack to cool completely.

STRAWBERRY MUFFINS

INGREDIENTS

1 cup (200g, 7oz) fresh strawberries

2/3 cup (140g, 5oz) caster sugar

1/3 cup (80ml, 3fl oz) vegetable oil

2 eggs

1½ cup (185g, 6oz) plain flour

½ tsp baking soda

½ tsp salt

18 fresh strawberries, halved, to decorate

METHOD

1. Heat oven to 220°C (425°F, Gas Mark 7). Line a 12-hole muffin tin with paper cases.

2. Smash strawberries to a rough pulp in large bowl with a fork or potato masher. Add sugar, oil and eggs and stir until thoroughly combined. Add the dry ingredients and stir again until all ingredients are just wet and combined.

3. Spoon batter into muffin cups filling two-thirds full. Poke 3 strawberry halves into the top of each muffin, ensuring they protrude from the batter.

4. Place in the oven and bake for 20 minutes or until a skewer inserted in the centre comes out clean.

5. Remove from oven and cool for 5 minutes before transferring to a wire rack to cool completely.

Note: Frozen strawberries can be used in place of fresh. Drain and pat dry with paper towel before using.

CINNAMON APPLE MUFFINS

INGREDIENTS

2½ cups (310g, 10oz)
plain flour

1 tbsp baking powder

1½ tsps ground cinnamon

1 cup (155g, 5oz)
brown sugar, firmly packed

2 medium apples,
peeled and roughly
chopped

¾ cup (120g, 4oz)
raisins

125g (4oz) butter,
melted, cooled

2 eggs, lightly whisked

¾ cup (185ml, 6fl oz)
milk

METHOD

1. Preheat oven to 200°C (390°F, Gas Mark 6) and line a 12-hole muffin tray with muffin cases.

2. Sift flour, baking powder and cinnamon together into a large bowl. Stir in brown sugar, apples and raisins and mix until well combined.

3. Whisk the butter, eggs and milk with a hand whisk until well combined.

4. Add the wet ingredients to the dry ingredients and stir with a large metal spoon until just combined. Do not over-mix.

5. Spoon the mixture evenly into the muffin cases.

6. Place in the oven and bake the muffins for 20 minutes or until golden and a skewer inserted in the centre comes out clean.

7. Remove from oven and stand for 5 minutes before turning onto a wire rack to cool completely.

APRICOT MUFFINS

INGREDIENTS

1 cup (160g, 6oz) dried apricots, chopped

125g (4oz) butter

1 cup (220g, 8oz) caster sugar

1 cup (250ml, 8fl oz) sour cream

2 cups (250g, 8oz) plain flour

1 tsp bicarbonate of soda

½ tsp salt

METHOD

1. Preheat oven to 200°C (390°F, Gas Mark 6). Line a 12-hole muffin tray and fill with muffin liners.

2. Soak apricots in boiling water for 5 minutes. Remove from heat.

3. Using an electric mixer, cream together butter and sugar until light and fluffy. Next add sour cream and mix well to combine.

4. Place dry ingredients in a bowl and mix together.

5. Add dry ingredients into creamed mixture and gently stir to combine.

6. Drain apricots and pat dry with paper towel. Stir apricots into batter. Spoon batter into paper cases.

7. Place in the oven and bake for 20 minutes until a skewer inserted into the centre comes out clean.

8. Stand in tray for 5 minutes. Transfer to a wire rack to cool. Serve.

CHOCOLATE MUFFINS

INGREDIENTS

2½ cups (310g, 10oz)
self-raising flour, sifted

¾ cup (90g, 3oz)
cocoa powder, sifted

1 cup (220g, 8oz)
caster sugar

¾ cup (120g, 4oz)
dark chocolate chips

½ cup (125ml,
4fl oz) vegetable oil

²/₃ cup (160ml, 5fl oz)
milk

1 tsp vanilla extract

2 eggs

METHOD

1. Preheat oven to 180°C (350°F, Gas Mark 4). Line a 12-hole muffin tray and fill with muffin liners.

2. Combine flour, cocoa, sugar and chocolate chips in a large bowl. Make a well in centre.

3. Whisk vegetable oil, milk, vanilla and eggs in a large jug. Pour oil mixture into well of dry ingredients. Using a metal spoon, stir gently until just combined. Spoon mixture into paper cases.

4. Place in the oven and bake for 25 minutes or until a skewer inserted into the centre comes out clean.

5. Stand in tray for 5 minutes. Transfer to a wire rack to cool. Serve.

SERVES 6 ★ PREP 25min ★ COOK TIME 15min

EASY CHEESY SCONES

INGREDIENTS

1¾ cups (215g, 7oz)
self-raising flour

Pinch of salt

Pinch of cayenne pepper

1 tsp baking powder

55g (2oz) butter, cubed

100g (3½ oz) cheddar
cheese, grated

⅓ cup (80ml, 3fl oz)
milk

Grated cheese,
for topping

METHOD

1. Preheat oven to 200°C (390°F, Gas Mark 6) and line a baking tray with greaseproof paper. Place into the oven to warm.

2. In a medium mixing bowl sift together flour, salt, cayenne pepper and baking powder.

3. Add butter to the bowl and rub with fingertips until a fine breadcrumb consistency forms. Sprinkle the grated cheese into the breadcrumb mixture and quickly combine until the cheese is mixed through.

4. Make a well in the centre of the mixture and pour in half of the milk. Stir to give a fairly soft but firm dough. Add more milk as required to reach the right consistency.

5. Roll out the dough on a lightly floured surface to approximately 2cm (1in) thick. Cut out the scones with a medium cutter and then place on the hot oven tray. Glaze the tops with extra milk and sprinkle cheese on the top of each scone.

6. Place in oven and bake for 15 minutes until golden brown.

ORANGE AND POPPY SEED FRIANDS

INGREDIENTS

185g (6oz) butter

1 cup (155g, 5oz) icing sugar

1 cup (120g, 4oz) almond meal

½ cup (60g, 2oz) plain flour, sifted

¼ cup (45g, 2oz) poppy seeds

2 oranges, zested

6 egg whites

Syrup

1 cup (220g, 8oz) sugar

1 cup (250ml, 8fl oz) water

½ cup (125ml, 4fl oz) orange juice

Peel from 1 orange, very finely sliced

METHOD

1. Preheat oven to 180°C (350°F, Gas Mark 4) and line a 12-hole friand tin with greaseproof paper.

2. Melt butter in a small saucepan over medium heat.

3. In a large mixing bowl, combine icing sugar, almond meal, flour, poppy seeds and orange zest. Stir in melted butter until just combined.

4. In an electric mixer, whisk egg-whites on low to medium speed until frothy. Using a metal spoon, fold through almond mixture.

5. Place mixture in prepared tin, dividing equally. Place in oven and bake 25 minutes, until a skewer inserted in the centre comes out clean. Remove from oven and leave in tin.

6. Meanwhile, make the sugar syrup. In a small saucepan over a low heat, combine syrup ingredients. Heat until sugar dissolves, then bring to boil and bubble for 30 seconds. Reduce heat and simmer, without stirring, for 5 minutes or until syrup has reduced slightly and thickened.

7. Prepare a wire rack with a board or greaseproof paper underneath to catch any drips. Remove friands from tin and place on wire tack. Pierce each friand 3-4 times with a metal skewer. Slowly pour over warm syrup, allowing to soak into friands. Serve immediately.

BLUEBERRY MUFFINS

INGREDIENTS

3 cups (375g, 12oz)
self-raising flour

1 tsp baking powder

1 cup (220g, 8oz)
caster sugar

½ cup (125ml, 4fl oz)
vegetable oil

1 egg

½ cup (125ml, 4fl oz)
milk

1 tsp vanilla extract

3 cups (300g, 10oz)
fresh or frozen blueberries

24 fresh blueberries,
to decorate

METHOD

1. Preheat oven to 180°C (350°F, Gas Mark 4). Line a 12-hole muffin tray and fill with muffin liners.

2. Sift the flour, baking powder and sugar into a large mixing bowl. Create a well in the centre.

3. Place oil, egg, milk and vanilla in a separate bowl and whisk until frothy and fully combined.

4. Pour wet ingredients into the well of the dry ingredients and mix until just combined. Add the blueberries and stir until combined. Spoon mixture into cases to about two-thirds full.

5. Place in oven and bake for 35 minutes or until a skewer inserted in the centre comes out clean. Remove from tray and sit for 5 minutes before transferring to a wire rack to cool completely.

6. Decorate with fresh blueberries before serving.

SERVES 16 ★ PREP 25MIN ★ COOK TIME 20MIN

CLASSIC SCONES

INGREDIENTS

3½ cups (435g, 14oz) self-raising flour

Pinch of salt

60g (2oz) chilled butter, chopped

1¼ cups (310ml, 10fl oz) milk, cold

Jam and clotted cream, to serve

METHOD

1. Preheat oven to 220°C (430°F, Gas Mark 7). Dust a baking tray with flour.

2. Combine flour and a pinch of salt in a bowl. Rub the butter into the flour mixture using fingertips until it resembles fine breadcrumbs. Make a well in centre and pour in 1 cup (250ml, 8fl oz) of the milk. Stir gently with metal spoon and add more milk as required to form a loose dough. When formed use hands to gently bring the dough together.

3. Turn dough onto floured surface. Knead gently for 30 seconds or until just smooth. Press or roll dough to a 2cm (1in) thickness. Use cutter to create 12 circles. Press leftover dough together. Repeat to make 4 more circles. Place scones close together on the prepared tray. Brush with extra milk.

4. Bake for 20 minutes or until risen and golden. Transfer to a wire rack to cool. Slice and serve with jam and cream.

SERVES 16 ★ PREP 25MIN ★ COOK TIME 20MIN

CHOCOLATE CHIP SCONES

INGREDIENTS

3½ cups (435g, 14oz) plain flour, sifted

½ cup (110g, 4oz) sugar

4 tsps baking powder

¼ tsp salt

340g (12oz) dark chocolate chips

2 cups (500ml, 1pt) thickened cream

2 tbsps melted butter, to finish

METHOD

1. Preheat oven to 190°C (375°F, Gas Mark 5). Line two baking trays with greaseproof paper.

2. In a large bowl, combine flour, sugar, baking powder and salt. Stir in chocolate chips.

3. Using a wooden spoon, stir cream into the flour mixture, stirring until ingredients are just wet and combined.

4. Turn the mixture out onto a lightly floured surface. Knead gently for 2 minutes or less until a soft dough forms. Divide the dough into two. Working with one piece at a time, pat each into an circle about 3cm (1in) thick and cut into 8 triangles. Transfer triangles onto baking trays, leaving a space between them.

5. Place in the oven and bake for 20 minutes or until lightly browned. Remove and place on a wire rack to cool.

6. Serve warm or at room temperature.

CHOCOLATE ALMOND MUFFINS

INGREDIENTS

2 cups (250g, 8oz)
plain flour

²/₃ cup (70g, 2½ oz) cocoa
powder

½ cup (110g, 4oz)
sugar

1½ tsp baking powder

½ tsp salt

²/₃ cup (80g, 3oz) almonds,
sliced

⅓ cup (80ml, 3fl oz)
vegetable oil

¾ cup (185ml, 6fl oz)
milk

½ tsp almond extract
or 1 tsp essence

1 egg, beaten

60g (2oz) butter

125g (4oz) cooking
chocolate, chopped

¼ cup (30g, 1oz)
chopped almonds,
to decorate

METHOD

1. Preheat oven to 200°C (400°F, Gas Mark 6). Line a 12-hole muffin tin with paper cases.

2. In a medium bowl, sift flour and cocoa powder together. Add sugar, baking powder, salt and almonds.

3. In a large bowl, whisk together oil, milk, almond extract and egg until light and well combined. Add dry ingredients and stir just until combined. Spoon into prepared cased, filling the muffin cups two-thirds full.

4. Place in the oven and bake for 20 minutes, or until a skewer inserted into the centre comes out clean.

5. Combine butter and chocolate in a heatproof bowl over a saucepan of simmering water, stirring constantly. When just melted, remove from the heat. Allow to cool slightly.

6. To decorate, pour over chocolate sauce and sprinkle with chopped almonds.

SERVES 6 ★ PREP 15MIN ★ COOK TIME 20MIN

COCONUT MUFFINS

INGREDIENTS

1 egg

½ tsp salt

2 tsps baking powder

½ cup (110g, 4oz) sugar

1 cup (90g, 3oz) coconut, shredded

2 cups (250g, 8oz) plain flour

½ cup (125ml, 4fl oz) milk

¼ cup (60ml, 2fl oz) oil

1 tsp vanilla essence

METHOD

1. Preheat oven to 180°C (350°F, Gas Mark 4) and line a 12-hole muffin tray with paper cases.

2. Beat egg in a small bowl.

3. Put salt, baking powder, sugar, coconut and flour in a large bowl.

4. Put the egg, milk, oil and essence into a large mixing bowl and mix until well combined. Add the dry ingredients and mix well. Spoon batter into paper cases filling to two-thirds.

5. Place in oven and bake for 20 minutes or until a skewer inserted in the centre comes out clean.

6. Remove from the oven, allow to stand for 5 minutes before cooling completely on a wire rack.

PEACH AND GINGER MUFFINS

INGREDIENTS

2 cups (250g, 8oz) plain flour

1 tbsp baking powder

1 tsp ground ginger

½ cup (125ml, 4fl oz) vegetable oil

½ cup (110g, 4oz) sugar

2 eggs

1 tsp vanilla

1 tbsp lemon rind

¾ cup (185ml, 6fl oz) milk

2 peaches, peeled and diced

Icing sugar, to dust

METHOD

1. Preheat oven to 190°C (375°F, Gas Mark 5) and line a 12-hole muffin tray with paper cases.

2. Sift the flour, baking powder and ginger over a large bowl. Set aside.

3. Using an electric mixer, in a separate bowl beat oil, sugar, eggs and vanilla. Stir in the lemon rind.

4. Add half the flour mixture to the egg mixture followed by half the milk. Repeat, mixing after each addition. Don't over-mix, just enough to make a smooth batter. Gently stir in the chopped peaches. Spoon batter into paper cases filling to two-thirds.

5. Place in the oven and bake for 25 minutes, or until the muffins are brown on top and a skewer inserted in the centre comes out clean.

6. Remove from oven and stand for 5 minutes before cooling completely on a wire rack. Dust with icing sugar.

CRANBERRY MUFFINS

INGREDIENTS

2½ cups (310g, 10oz) flour

2 tsps baking powder

¼ tsp salt

1¼ cup (275g, 10oz) sugar

115g (4oz) butter, room temperature

2 eggs

½ cup (125ml, 4fl oz) milk

2 cups (320g, 12oz) cranberries, coarsely chopped

METHOD

1. Preheat oven to 180°C (350°F, Gas Mark 4) and line a 12-hole muffin tray with paper cases.

2. Stir together flour, baking powder and salt in a medium mixing bowl. Set aside.

3. Using an electric mixer, cream sugar and butter together in a medium bowl until light and fluffy. Add eggs one at a time, beating after each addition. Add half the flour mixture followed by half the milk. Repeat, mixing after each addition. Don't over-mix, just enough to make a smooth batter. Stir in cranberries. Spoon into paper cases, filling two-thirds full with batter.

5. Place in oven and bake for 20 minutes, or until the muffins are brown on top and a skewer inserted in the centre comes out clean.

6. Remove from oven, allow to stand for 5 minutes before cooling completely on a wire rack.

BANANA MUFFINS

INGREDIENTS

1¾ cups (215g, 7oz) plain flour

½ tsp baking powder

1 tsp bicarbonate of soda

½ tsp nutmeg

½ tsp salt

3 ripe bananas, mashed

¾ cup (165g, 6oz) caster sugar

1 egg

80g (3oz) butter, melted

METHOD

1. Preheat oven to 180°C (350°F, Gas Mark 4) and line a 12-hole muffin tray with paper cases.

2. Sift together the flour, baking powder, bicarb soda, nutmeg and salt in a medium mixing bowl. Set aside.

3. Combine mashed bananas, sugar, egg and melted butter in a large mixing bowl. Gradually fold in dry ingredient mix, and combine with a metal spoon until smooth. Spoon into paper cases, filling two-thirds full with batter.

4. Place in oven and bake for 20 minutes, or until the muffins are brown on top and a skewer inserted in the centre comes out clean.

5. Remove from oven, allow to stand for 5 minutes before cooling completely on a wire rack.

EASY FRUIT SCONES

INGREDIENTS

4 cups (500g, 1lb)
self-raising flour

2 tsp baking powder

1 cup (160g, 6oz)
sultanas

4 tbsps butter, chopped

1½ cups (375ml, 13fl oz)
milk

Icing sugar, to dust

METHOD

1. Preheat oven to 210°C (410°F, Gas Mark 6). Grease and flour a baking tray.

2. Sift flour and baking powder over a large bowl. Mix in sultanas.

3. Add the butter and rub through evenly into the mix using fingertips until a rough crumble forms.

4. Make a well in the centre and add milk. Mix together with a fork, combining to create a sticky dough.

5. Scrape the mixture onto a flat and lightly dusted surface. Fold the mixture in on itself a few times and quickly knead to combine.

6. Use a floured knife to cut into 12 even pieces. Gently roll each piece with floured hands and place evenly on the baking tray, leaving a small gap between the scones.

7. Place in oven and bake for 20 minutes until golden brown.

8. Remove from oven and transfer to a wire rack to cool.

9. Dust with icing sugar before serving warm or at room temperature.

LEMON MUFFINS

INGREDIENTS

Muffins

1⅓ cups (290g, 10½ oz) sugar

2 lemons, zested

2 eggs

¼ cup (60ml, 2fl oz) olive oil

⅔ cup (160ml, 5fl oz) milk

1 cup (125g, 4oz) plain flour

½ tsp baking powder

½ tsp salt

Glaze

1½ cups (235g, 8oz) icing sugar

2 lemons, juiced

2 tbsps butter, melted

¼ cup (40g, 1½ oz) candied lemon peel, thinly sliced

METHOD

1. Preheat oven to 180°C (350°F, Gas Mark 4) and lightly grease a 12-hole fluted mini muffin tin with butter.

2. Combine sugar and lemon zest in the bowl of an electric mixer. With the mixer set on medium, add one egg, then gradually pour in the olive oil and milk. Add the other egg, pulsing for 30 seconds until a thin batter forms.

3. Sift flour, baking powder and salt over a small bowl. Add to the blender in 2 batches, pulsing lightly until just combined. Pour batter into the prepared tin.

4. Place in oven and bake for 25 minutes or until muffins spring back when lightly touched. Remove from oven and cool in the tin for 10 minutes, then loosen the sides with a knife and invert the cakes onto a wire rack to cool.

5. Meanwhile, whisk icing sugar, lemon juice and butter until smooth, adding more lemon juice if required to thin the mixture. Drizzle over the warm cakes and garnish with candied lemon peel.

CHEESY MUSHROOM MUFFINS

INGREDIENTS

1¼ cups (310ml, 10fl oz) milk

1 egg

¾ cup (185ml, 6fl oz) olive oil

3 cups (375g, 12oz) self-raising flour

²/₃ cup Parmesan cheese, grated

15 mushrooms, diced

3 tbsps basil, finely chopped (optional)

METHOD

1. Preheat the oven to 200°C (390°F, Gas Mark 6) and line a 12-hole muffin tray with paper cases.

2. In a small bowl, whisk milk, egg and oil together.

3. Sift flour over a large mixing bowl. Add cheese, mushrooms and basil, if using. Make a well in the centre.

4. Slowly pour milk, egg and oil mix into the well and fold gently to combine. Spoon into paper cases, filling two-thirds full with batter.

5. Place in oven and bake for 20 minutes, or until the muffins are brown on top and a skewer inserted in the centre comes out clean.

6. Remove from the oven, allow to stand for 5 minutes before cooling completely on a wire rack.

SPICED PUMPKIN MUFFINS

INGREDIENTS

2 cups (250g, 8oz) plain flour

2 tsps baking powder

1 tsp cinnamon

½ tsp ground ginger

¼ tsp nutmeg

¼ tsp ground cloves

½ tsp salt

6 tbsps butter

1⅓ cup (205g, 7oz) light brown sugar

2 eggs

1⅓ cups (300g, 10oz) pumpkin, boiled and pureed

1 tsp vanilla extract

METHOD

1. Preheat oven to 180°C (350°F, Gas Mark 4). Line a 12-hole muffin tray with paper cases. In a medium bowl, combine flour, baking powder, cinnamon, ginger, nutmeg, cloves and salt. Set aside.

2. Using an electric mixer on high speed, cream together butter and sugar until light and fluffy. Add the eggs, one at a time, beating after each addition.

3. Add the pumpkin puree and vanilla extract and mix to combine. Stir in the dry ingredients, mixing until just combined. Spoon the batter into the prepared paper cases so they are two-thirds of the way full.

4. Place in oven and bake for 20 minutes. The muffins are done when the tops looked cracked and golden brown and a skewer inserted in the centre comes out clean.

5. Remove from the oven, allow to stand for 5 minutes before cooling completely on a wire rack.

FLOURLESS ZUCCHINI CHOCOLATE MUFFINS

INGREDIENTS

1 cup (170g, 6oz) zucchini, grated

½ cup (180g, 6oz) smooth peanut butter

1 very ripe banana

1 egg

¼ cup (90g, 3oz) honey

¼ cup (30g, 1oz) cocoa powder

2 tbsps ground flaxseed (or chia seeds)

1 tsp vanilla extract

½ tsp baking soda

¾ cup (120g, 4oz) chocolate chips

METHOD

1. Preheat oven to 190°C (375°F, Gas Mark 5) and lightly grease a 6-hole muffin tray.

2. Squeeze zucchini and drain off excess water. Repeat. Set aside.

3. Place peanut butter, banana, egg, honey, cocoa powder, flaxseed, vanilla extract and baking soda in a blender or food processor, and blend until a smooth batter forms. Stir in zucchini and a third of the chocolate chips.

4. Pour batter into prepared tray about two-thirds of the way full. Sprinkle remaining chocolate chips on top.

5. Place in oven and bake for 35 minutes or until the tops are set and a skewer inserted into the centre comes out clean.

SWEET POTATO AND SPINACH MUFFINS

INGREDIENTS

150g (5oz) baby spinach (or 1 bunch fresh spinach)

1½ cups (185g, 6oz) plain flour

3 tsps baking powder

1 large sweet potato, peeled and grated

½ cup (80g, 3oz) sun-dried tomatoes, chopped

⅓ cup (40g, 1½ oz) Parmesan cheese, finely grated

2 eggs

⅓ cup (80ml, 3fl oz) milk

2 tbsps olive oil

METHOD

1. Preheat oven to 180°C (350°F, Gas Mark 4) and grease a 12-hole muffin tray.

2. Place spinach in a large bowl and cover with boiling water. Drain. When cool, squeeze out excess water and chop.

3. Sift flour and baking powder over a large bowl. Add spinach, grated sweet potato, sun-dried tomatoes and Parmesan cheese.

4. Whisk together eggs, milk and oil in a separate bowl.

5. Add wet ingredients to dry ingredients and stir until just combined, being careful not to over-mix. Spoon mixture into muffin tray to two-thirds of the way full.

6. Bake for 20 minutes or until golden in colour and a skewer inserted into the centre comes out clean.

PEAR AND GINGER MUFFINS

INGREDIENTS

60g (4oz) butter, room temperature

½ cup (80g, 3oz) packed brown sugar

¼ cup (55g, 2oz) sugar

2 eggs

1 tsp vanilla extract

1¼ cup (155g, 5oz) plain flour

1¼ cup (155g, 5oz) whole wheat flour

2 tsps baking powder

2 tsps ground cinnamon

½ tsp ground ginger

¼ tsp ground nutmeg

½ tsp salt

½ cup (125ml, 4fl oz) milk

2 medium-sized pears, peeled and diced

½ cup (80g, 3oz) chopped candied ginger

½ cup (60g, 2oz) chopped nuts

METHOD

1. Preheat oven to 200°C (400°F, Gas Mark 6). Line a 12-hole muffin tray with paper cases.

2. Using an electric mixer on high speed, cream together butter and sugars until light and fluffy. Add the eggs, one at a time, beating after each addition. Add vanilla extract and beat to combine.

3. In a separate bowl combine flours, baking powder, spice and salt.

4. With the electric mixer on low speed, add a third of flour mixture into creamed mixture followed by a third of the milk. Continue alternating between the flour and the milk, mixing just until the flour is incorporated. Add the diced pears, candied ginger and nuts and gently fold into the batter. Divide batter between the muffin cups and fill to the top

5. Place in the oven and bake for 20 minutes. The muffins are done when the tops looked cracked and a skewer inserted in the centre comes out clean.

6. Remove from the oven, allow to stand for 5 minutes before cooling completely on a wire rack.

SPINACH AND FETA MUFFINS

INGREDIENTS

2½ cups (310g, 10oz) flour

1 tsp baking powder

½ tsp salt

1 cup (250ml, 8fl oz) milk

½ cup (125ml, 4fl oz) oil

2 eggs

250g (9oz) frozen spinach, thawed and drained

100g (3½ oz) feta, chopped

75g (3oz) feta, cubed

METHOD

1. Preheat oven to 180°C (350°F, Gas Mark 4)°F. Line a 12-hole muffin tray with paper cases.

2. Sift flour, baking powder and salt over a large bowl. Add milk, oil and eggs and whisk until well combined. Add the spinach and feta and mix until well combined. Spoon the batter into the prepared paper cases so they are two-thirds of the way full. Dot feta cubes on top, pressing gently into batter.

3. Place in the oven and bake for 20 minutes. The muffins are done when the tops looked cracked and golden brown and when a skewer inserted in the centre comes out clean.

4. Remove from the oven, allow to stand for 5 minutes before cooling completely on a wire rack.

BREAKFAST MUFFINS

INGREDIENTS

1½ cups (185g, 6oz)
plain flour

1¼ cup (155g, 5oz)
toasted muesli

1 tsp ground cinnamon

1 tsp bicarbonate
of soda

¾ cup (120g, 4oz)
firmly packed brown sugar

½ cup (30g, 1oz)
quinoa flakes (or oats)

¾ cup (120g, 4oz)
dates, chopped

1½ cups (375ml,
13fl oz) buttermilk

½ cup (125ml, 4fl oz)
vegetable oil

1 egg, beaten

METHOD

1. Preheat oven to 200°C (390°F, Gas Mark 6). Line a 12-hole muffin tray with paper cases.

2. Combine all ingredients in large bowl, stir until just combined. Transfer to the fridge and chill for 2 hours.

3. Spoon the batter into the prepared paper cases so they are two-thirds of the way full.

4. Place in the oven and bake for 20 minutes. The muffins are done when the tops looked cracked and golden brown and when a skewer inserted in the centre comes out clean.

5. Remove from the oven, allow to stand for 5 minutes before cooling completely on a wire rack.

PUMPKIN WALNUT SCONES

INGREDIENTS

3 cups (375g, 12oz)
plain flour

⅓ cup (70g, 2½ oz)
sugar

1 tbsp baking powder

¾ tsp salt

¾ tsp cinnamon

½ tsp nutmeg

½ tsp allspice

125g (4oz) butter,
chilled and cubed

1 cup (125g, 4oz)
walnuts, finely chopped

⅔ cup (150g, 5oz)
pumpkin, mashed

2 eggs

Walnut halves,
to decorate

METHOD

1. Line a baking tray with greaseproof paper.

2. In a large mixing bowl, combine flour, sugar, baking powder, salt and spices. Add butter to the dry ingredients rubbing with fingertips to create a coarse crumb. Add the walnuts, mixing by hand until just blended.

3. In a separate bowl, beat the mashed pumpkin and eggs together well. Add wet ingredients to the dry ingredients and bring the dough together with your hands.

4. Place dough onto a sheet of greaseproof paper and flatten using your hands or a rolling pin until 3cm (1in) thick. Cut into eight triangles and lay the individual scones on lined tray.

5. Transfer to the freezer for 30 minutes.

6. Preheat oven to 220°C (430°F, Gas Mark 7) 10 minutes before scones are due out of the freezer.

7. Remove from the freezer and lightly press walnut halves into the top of each scone.

8. Place in oven and bake for 20-25 minutes, until a skewer inserted into the centre comes out clean.

9. Remove from oven, allow to stand for 5 minutes before cooling completely on a wire rack.

RASPBERRY AND WHITE CHOCOLATE SCONES

INGREDIENTS

3 cups (375g, 12oz) plain flour

½ cup (110g, 4oz) sugar

6 tsps baking powder

½ tsp salt

175g (6oz) cold butter, cubed

180g (6oz) white chocolate, chopped

2 tbsps lemon juice

2 tsps vanilla extract

1 cup (250ml, 8fl oz) milk

1½ cups (185g, 6oz) frozen raspberries

1 egg, beaten with a little water (egg wash)

Whipped cream and fresh raspberries, to decorate

METHOD

1. Preheat oven to 190°C (375°F, Gas Mark 5) and line a baking tray with greaseproof paper.

2. In a food processor, combine flour, sugar, baking powder and salt. Pulse in the cold butter until this mixture resembles a coarse crumb.

3. Transfer to a large bowl and stir in the white chocolate.

4. Mix together the lemon juice, vanilla extract and milk.

5. Pour half of the liquid over the the dry mixture. Bring together gently with a fork, adding more liquid as required to form a soft dough ball. When the flour is almost incorporated, add the frozen raspberries. Combine as lightly as possible.

6. Roll dough to 2.5cm (1in) thickness and cut out scones with a cutter or in rectangles with a sharp knife. Place scones on baking tray and brush the tops of the scones with egg wash.

7. Place in oven and bake for 25 minutes or until light golden brown.

8. Remove from the oven, allow to stand for 5 minutes before cooling completely on a wire rack.

9. Serve with whipped cream and fresh raspberries.

SERVES 12 ★ PREP 20min ★ COOK TIME 20min

COCONUT CHOC-CHIP MUFFINS

INGREDIENTS

2½ cups (310g, 10oz)
self-raising flour

1 cup (220g, 8oz)
caster sugar

½ cup (40g, 1½ oz)
shredded coconut

1 cup (155g, 5oz)
dark chocolate chips

1 egg

½ cup (125ml, 4fl oz)
vegetable oil

¾ cup (185ml, 6fl oz)
milk

1 tsp vanilla essence

METHOD

1. Preheat oven to 200°C (390°F, Gas Mark 6). Line a 12-hole muffin tray with paper cases.

2. Sift flour and sugar over a large bowl. Add coconut and chocolate chips and stir to combine.

3. Whisk egg in a small bowl. Add oil, milk and vanilla and whisk again until well combined.

4. Add wet mixture to dry ingredients and fold through gently until the flour is combined.

5. Pour batter into cases to two-thirds full.

6. Place in oven and bake for 20 minutes until a skewer inserted in the centre comes out clean.

7. Remove from oven, allow to stand for 5 minutes before cooling completely on a wire rack.

SAVOURY POTATO MUFFINS

INGREDIENTS

1¾ cups (215g, 7oz) flour

3 tsps baking powder

¼ tsp salt

½ tsp freshly ground black pepper

2 tbsps fresh basil, chopped

1 cup (125g, 4oz) cheddar cheese, grated

1 cup (325g, 12oz) potato, mashed

½ cup (125ml, 4fl oz) sour cream

½ cup (125ml, 4fl oz) milk

2 eggs, lightly beaten

Sesame seeds, to garnish

METHOD

1. Preheat oven to 180°C (350°F, Gas Mark 4) and lightly grease a 12-hole muffin tray.

2. Sift flour, baking powder, salt and pepper over a large bowl. Add basil, cheese and potato and mix to combine. Add sour cream, milk and eggs and stir until just combined.

3. Spoon batter into each of the muffin cups filling two-thirds of the way. Sprinkle the tops of the muffins with sesame seeds.

4. Place in oven and bake for 20 minutes, until the muffins have risen and a skewer inserted in the centre comes out clean.

★

TARTS
AND
PIES

★

APPLE TARTE TATIN

INGREDIENTS

1¾ cup (275g, 9oz) brown sugar

150g (5oz) butter, sliced

2½ kg (5lb 8oz) apples, peeled, cored and halved

2 sheets puff pastry

METHOD

1. Spread sugar over the base of a medium sized oven-proof frying pan. Place butter slices evenly over the top.

2. Arrange apple halves on their sides, facing in one direction to create concentric circles. Pack the apples closely together.

3. Place the frying pan over a medium-low heat on the stove and cook, uncovered, for 1-1½ hours until the sugar turns golden brown and covers the apples with caramel. Adjust the heat up or down to keep the sauce at a gentle simmer.

4. Preheat the oven to 220°C (425°F, Gas Mark 7).

5. Remove pastry from the freezer to thaw. Place the pastry over the apples, gently stretching it to tuck into the sides of the frying pan.

6. Put the frying pan in the oven (on a baking tray to catch juices) and bake for 20 minutes until pastry is golden brown.

7. Remove from the oven and immediately invert onto a large serving plate.

LEMON MERINGUE PIE

INGREDIENTS

Pastry

1¾ cups (215g, 7oz) plain flour

1 tbsp icing sugar

140g (5oz) butter, chilled and coarsely chopped

1 egg yolk

2 tbsps iced water

Filling

½ cup (75g, 3oz) cornflour

1½ cups (330g, 12oz) caster sugar

½ cup (125ml, 4fl oz) lemon juice

1¼ cups (310ml, 10fl oz) water

2 tsps lemon rind, finely grated

80g (3oz) butter, coarsely chopped

3 eggs, separated

METHOD

1. Rub flour, icing sugar and butter together with fingertips until crumbly. Add egg yolk and iced water. Mix until ingredients come together. Knead dough on floured surface until smooth. Form into a ball and wrap in plastic wrap. Refrigerate for 30 minutes.

2. Grease a 24cm (9½ in) springform fluted flan tin. Roll pastry large enough to line tin. Using a rolling pin, fold pastry into pan. Press pastry gently into base and sides and trim edge with a sharp knife. Cover with plastic wrap and refrigerate for 30 minutes.

3. Preheat oven to 200°C (390°F, Gas Mark 6). Blind bake for 15 minutes. Remove paper and weights from pastry case. Bake for a further 10 minutes until golden. Remove and set aside to cool.

4. Combine cornflour and 1 cup (220g, 8oz) caster sugar in a medium saucepan. Gradually stir in lemon juice and water and stir until smooth. Cook over a high heat until mixture boils and then thickens. Reduce heat and simmer, stirring, for 1 minute. Remove from heat. Stir in rind and butter and, quickly, stir in egg yolks. Set aside to cool for 10 minutes.

5. Spoon filling into the pastry case and spread evenly across base. Cover and refrigerate for 2 hours.

6. Preheat oven to 220°C (430°F, Gas Mark 7).

7. Beat egg whites with electric mixer until soft peaks form. Slowly add remaining sugar, beating until sugar dissolves and glossy, firm peaks form.

8. Spread meringue mixture onto lemon filling. Bake for 2 minutes or until meringue is golden brown.

SERVES 8 ★ PREP 40MIN (PLUS CHILLING) ★ COOK TIME 1HR 15MIN

CHERRY PIE

INGREDIENTS

Pastry

3 cups (375g, 12oz) plain flour

1 tbsp sugar

¾ tsp salt

250g (9oz) chilled butter, cubed

5 tbsps iced water

Filling

1 cup (220g, 8oz) sugar

3 tbsps cornflour

¼ tsp salt

5 cups (775g, 25oz) whole pitted sour cherries

30g (1oz) butter, chopped

1 tsp fresh lemon juice

½ tsp vanilla extract

To finish

2 tbsp milk

1 tbsp sugar

METHOD

1. Combine flour, sugar, and salt in a large bowl. Add butter and rub using fingertips until loosely crumbled. Add iced water and bring dough together with hands. Add more water if dough is too dry to combine well. Roll into a ball and divide into two pieces. Wrap in plastic wrap and place in the fridge for at least 30 minutes.

2. Preheat oven to 220°C (425°F, Gas Mark 7) and grease a 23cm (9in) glass pie dish.

3. Combine sugar, cornflour and salt in a mixing bowl to blend. Stir in cherries, chopped butter, lemon juice and vanilla. Set aside.

4. Roll out two dough discs on floured surface, each to 30cm (12in) round. Transfer one disc to fill the bottom and sides of the pie dish. With a sharp knife, trim overhang. Spoon filling on top of pastry base creating a slight mound in the centre.

5. Place second dough disc on floured surface and using a large knife or pastry wheel cut ten strips of dough. Arrange dough strips on top of the filling, forming a lattice. Trim dough if required. Fold base crust over ends of strips and crimp edges to seal. Brush lattice crust with milk. Sprinkle lattice with sugar.

6. Place pie on a baking tray and bake for 15 minutes. Reduce oven temperature to 190°C (375°F, Gas Mark 5) and continue to bake until filling is bubbling and crust is golden brown, approximately 1 hour.

7. Transfer pie to rack and cool completely.

ITALIAN RICOTTA TART

INGREDIENTS

Base

2 cups (250g, 8oz) plain flour

1 egg

120g (4oz) butter, cubed

30g (1oz) caster sugar

½ cup (80g, 3oz) icing sugar

¼ cup (30g, 1oz) almond meal

½ lemon, zested

Pinch of salt

Filling

⅓ cup (115g, 4oz) honey

½ cup (110g, 4oz) caster sugar

Pinch of salt

80g (3oz) butter

½ cup (125ml, 4fl oz) thickened cream

1 lemon, zested

2 tablespoons lemon juice

140g (5oz) ricotta

1 egg

1 cup (125g, 4oz) pine nuts

METHOD

1. Rub flour, egg, butter, sugars, almond meal, lemon zest and salt together with finger tips until a rough crumble forms. Shape into a ball, wrap in plastic wrap and refrigerate for 1 hour.

2. Grease and line a 23cm (9in) springform tart tin. Roll the dough, using the base of the tin as a guide for size. Place into the tin and press into the edges. Prick the bottom with a fork. Place in the freezer for 30 minutes.

3. Preheat oven to 190°C (375°F, Gas Mark 5).

4. Combine honey, sugar and salt in a medium saucepan over a low heat. Add butter and cook, stirring constantly, until butter has melted and sugar has dissolved. Remove from heat and set aside to cool for 15 minutes. Then add cream, lemon zest, lemon juice, ricotta and egg and combine smooth.

5. Remove pastry base from the freezer and scatter over most of the pine nuts. Pour in the filling and smooth over with a spatula. Scatter on a few more pine nuts.

6. Transfer to oven and bake for 50 minutes, or until the tart and crust are golden brown.

7. Remove from oven and leave to cool completely before removing from the tart tin.

SERVES 8 ★ PREP 40MIN ★ COOK TIME 40MIN

PUMPKIN PIE

INGREDIENTS

Pastry

3 cups (375g, 12oz)
plain flour

1 tsp salt

220g (8oz) chilled
butter, cubed

½ cup (125ml, 4fl oz)
iced water

Filling

2¼ cups (500g, 1lb 2oz)
pumpkin, mashed

1 x 400g (14oz) can
evapourated milk

2 eggs, beaten

1¼ cups (195g, 6½ oz)
soft dark brown sugar

½ tsp ground cinnamon

½ tsp ground ginger

½ tsp ground nutmeg

½ tsp salt

Whipped cream,
to serve

METHOD

1. Preheat oven to 200°C (390°F, Gas Mark 6).

2. Combine flour and salt in a mixing bowl. Rub butter into flour until a rough crumble forms. Gradually add iced water to mixture, stirring to combine, until dough is moist enough to hold together.

3. Grease a 20cm (8in) glass pie dish. Shape pastry into a ball. On a floured board, roll pastry out to about 5mm (¼ in) thick. Transfer to pie dish, gently pressing pastry into the base and up sides.

4. Using a sharp knife, cut off any excess around the rim, and press pastry to secure around the edge.

5. Using an electric mixer set on medium speed, beat pumpkin with evapourated milk, eggs, sugar, cinnamon, ginger, nutmeg and salt until well combined.

6. Spoon mixture into pie dish and bake in preheated oven for 40 minutes or until a skewer inserted in the centre comes out clean.

7. Serve with whipped cream.

PORTUGUESE CUSTARD TART

INGREDIENTS

2 egg yolks

1 whole egg

½ cup (110g, 4oz) caster sugar

1½ tbsps cornflour

1¼ cups (310ml, 10fl oz) milk

1 cup (250ml, 8fl oz) thickened cream

1½ tsps vanilla extract

1 tbsp caster sugar

2 tsps ground cinnamon

2-4 sheets frozen puff pastry, partially thawed

METHOD

1. Preheat oven to 210°C (410°F, Gas Mark 6). Grease a 12-hole muffin tin.

2. Whisk egg yolks, whole egg, sugar and cornflour in a medium saucepan until well combined. Slowly add the milk and then the cream, stirring to combine.

3. Turn heat on to low and cook the custard, stirring constantly with the whisk until it comes to a simmer and begins to thicken. Remove from heat and stir in the vanilla. Transfer custard to a heatproof bowl and cover surface with plastic wrap. Place in the fridge for 1 hour.

4. Combine sugar and cinnamon and sprinkle half of the mixture over one of the pastry sheets. Cover with the other pastry sheet and then sprinkle with remaining cinnamon sugar. Press the two sheets together using a rolling pin. Firmly roll the two sheets of pastry together into a log. Using a sharp knife, cut the pastry log into 12 even portions.

5. Place a pastry portion on a floured bench top. Flatten slightly then roll into a 10cm (4in) circle. Gently press the pastry round into a muffin tin hole. Repeat with the remaining pastry portions.

6. Spoon the cooled custard evenly into the pastry cases. Bake in preheated oven for 30 minutes or until the pastry is crisp and the custard golden on top.

7. Remove from oven and stand the tarts in tin for 5 minutes before transferring to a wire rack to cool completely. Serve at room temperature.

CHOCOLATE TART

INGREDIENTS

Sweet pastry

150g (5oz) butter,
room temperature

½ cup (110g, 4oz)
caster sugar

2 cups (250g, 8oz)
plain flour

¼ cup (30g, 1oz)
almond meal

1 egg yolk

Juice of ½ lemon

2 tsps vanilla extract

1 tbsp iced water

Filling

400g (14oz) dark chocolate,
finely chopped

1 cup (250ml, 8fl oz)
thickened cream

½ cup (125ml, 4fl oz)
milk

2 small eggs,
beaten

½ cup (60g, 2oz)
cocoa, for dusting

METHOD

1. In an electric mixer, beat butter and sugar together until light and fluffy. Add flour and almond meal and stir well to combine. Add egg yolk, lemon juice, vanilla and iced water and stir to combine. Shape dough with hands to form a disc shape. Wrap in plastic wrap and refrigerate for 1 hour.

2. Grease a 24cm (9½ in) fluted tart tin. Roll out pastry on a lightly floured surface to 5mm (¼ in) thick. Using the rolling pin, transfer pastry to the tin. Press gently around the base and trim edges with a sharp knife. Place in the fridge to chill for 30 minutes.

3. Preheat oven to 180°C (350°F, Gas Mark 4). Blind bake pastry for 5 minutes or until edges are golden. Remove paper and weights, and bake for 10 minutes until base is golden. Set aside.

4. Place chocolate in a bowl and set aside. Bring cream and milk to simmer in a saucepan over medium heat until bubbles just form at the edges. Then add to chocolate and allow to stand for 1-2 minutes until the chocolate just melts. Cool slightly, then stir in the beaten eggs.

5. Reduce oven to 130°C (265°F, Gas Mark 1). Pour chocolate mixture into tart and bake for 30-35 minutes.

6. Set aside to cool. Dust with cocoa before serving.

GRANDMA'S APPLE PIE

INGREDIENTS

Pastry

2 cups (250g, 8oz) plain flour

½ cup (60g, 2oz) self-raising flour

Pinch of salt

185g (6oz) butter, chilled, cut into small pieces

⅓ cup (70g, 2½ oz) caster sugar

2 eggs, beaten

1 tbsp iced water

1 tbsp milk

Caster sugar, to sprinkle

Filling

45g (1½ oz) unsalted butter

½ cup (110g, 4oz) caster sugar

8 large apples, peeled and chopped

1 tsp ground cinnamon

¼ tsp ground cloves

METHOD

1. Sift flours and salt into a large mixing bowl. Add butter and rub lightly into flour using fingertips. Continue until mixture resembles fine breadcrumbs, then stir through sugar. Combine half the beaten eggs with the iced water, and pour over the flour mixture.

2. Bring the dough together with your hands. Form into a ball, and divide into two pieces, one slightly bigger than the other. Wrap in plastic wrap, and chill in the fridge for 30 minutes.

3. Meanwhile, heat butter and sugar in a large frying pan over medium heat. When butter has melted, add apples and spices. Cook, stirring occasionally, for 10 minutes or until apples have softened. Set aside to cool.

4. Preheat oven to 180°C (350°F, Gas Mark 4) and prepare a 30cm (12in) shallow pie dish.

5. Roll out the bigger pastry ball on a floured workbench using the pie dish as a guide for size. Roll pastry around rolling pin, then unroll over pie dish. Press pastry into edges and allow overhang. Place filling in base. Roll the small pastry piece to a slightly smaller circle. Add milk to remaining beaten egg and brush around rim of pastry base. Place small pastry circle on top and press lightly to affix.

6. Trim excess pastry from edges with a sharp knife. Crimp edges of pastry together with using a fork or fingers. Chill in the fridge for 30 minutes.

7. Place pie dish on a baking tray. Brush top of pie with beaten egg mix and sprinkle with caster sugar. Cut a cross in the centre of the pie and bake for 45 minutes until golden.

CARAMEL NUTLETS

INGREDIENTS

Filling

²/₃ cup (160ml, 5fl oz) cream

2 tbsps water

²/₃ cup (140g, 5oz) sugar

25g (1oz) butter, chilled and cubed

Pinch of salt

½ cup (60g, 2oz) nuts

¼ cup (40g, 1½ oz) raisins

Sweet pastry

1¹/₃ cups (165g, 5½ oz) plain flour

¼ cup (55g, 2oz) sugar

85g (3oz) butter, room temperature

1 egg yolk

METHOD

1. Preheat oven to 190°C (375°F, Gas Mark 5).

2. Place cream in a small saucepan on medium heat. Gently bring to the boil and reduce heat to very low to keep warm.

3. Place water and sugar in a small saucepan and bring to the boil. Allow sugar to bubble gently and cook, without stirring, until sugar turns dark brown. Slowly pour in the warm cream, swirling the saucepan. Whisk if required. Add more cream to loosen thick caramel, if needed. Remove from heat and set aside to cool.

4. Sift flour and sugar in a bowl. Add diced butter and rub with fingertips until a crumbly consistency is achieved.Stir in egg yolk and the bring dough together with hands.

5. Divide dough into 4 equal parts, flatten, and line the bottom of four tartlet tins.

6. Blind bake the tart shells for 10 minutes.

7. Meanwhile, stir nuts and raisins into the caramel.

8. Remove tart shells from oven and remove paper and weights. Allow to cool slightly and then spoon the caramel mixture into each tartlet.

SERVES 4 ★ PREP 40MIN (PLUS CHILLING) ★ COOK TIME 25MIN

ORANGE CHOCOLATE TARTLETS

INGREDIENTS

Pastry

250g (9oz) butter, room temperature

¾ cup (165g, 6oz) caster sugar

2 eggs

4 cups (500g, 1lb) plain flour

Pinch of salt

1 egg, beaten

Filling

²/₃ cup (150ml, 5fl oz) thickened cream

1 orange, zested

150g (5oz) dark chocolate, grated

1 tbsp orange liqueur

Orange, very thinly sliced, to serve (optional)

METHOD

1. Using an electric mixer, cream butter and sugar until light and fluffy. Beat in the eggs one at a time and beat after each addition.

2. Sift flour and salt into a large bowl. Gradually add to the creamed mixture, stirring with a metal spoon after each addition. Using your hands, bring the dough together into a ball and knead lightly. Wrap in plastic wrap and chill for 1 hour.

3. Roll out the pastry and use to line individual tartlet tins. Cover and place in the fridge for 30 minutes.

4. Preheat the oven to 180°C (350°F, Gas Mark 4).

5. Blind bake for 10 minutes. Remove weights and paper, and return to the oven for a further 5 minutes until golden. Remove from the oven and set aside to cool.

6. Reduce the heat to 110°C (230°F, Gas Mark ¼). Brush the pastry cases with beaten egg. Return to the oven for 3-4 minutes until the glaze is set.

7. Heat the thickened cream in a small saucepan with orange zest. Heat until bubbles just start to form at the edges and then remove from the heat.

8. Pour cream over the grated chocolate, stirring until the chocolate has melted. Stir in the orange liqueur.

9. Garnish with whole orange slices, if desired.

SERVES 6 ★ PREP 40MIN (PLUS CHILLING) ★ COOK TIME 40MIN

BLUEBERRY PIE

INGREDIENTS

2½ cups (310g, 10oz) plain flour

Pinch of salt

¼ cup (55g, 2oz) caster sugar

225g (8oz, ½ lb) butter, chilled, chopped

⅓ cup (80ml, 3fl oz) iced water

3¾ cups (375g, 13oz) blueberries

1 tbsp cornflour

1 tsp lemon zest

1 egg, beaten

2 tbsps milk

METHOD

1. Add flour, salt and 2 tablespoons of the caster sugar to the mixing bowl of a food processor. Add butter and pulse until mixture resembles fine breadcrumbs. Add water and process until mixture just starts to form a dough.

2. Turn onto a floured surface. Knead until smooth. Divide the mixture into a third and two-thirds and roll into two balls. Wrap in plastic wrap and place in the fridge for 1 hour.

3. Grease a 23cm (9in) glass pie dish.

4. Meanwhile, combine the blueberries, cornflour, lemon zest and remaining caster sugar in a large bowl.

5. Preheat oven to 200°C (390°F, Gas Mark 6).

6. Mix beaten egg and milk together in a small bowl to form an eggwash. Set aside.

7. Roll out large pastry ball on a floured surface until 5mm (¼ in) thick. Using a rolling pin fold the pastry into the pie dish, allowing edges to overhang. Add blueberry filling.

8. Roll out smaller dough ball on a floured surface until 5mm (¼ inch) thick. Cut into strips. Brush edges of pie with eggwash. Arrange strips in a lattice pattern over the filling and press edges to seal. Trim edges with a sharp knife. Place in the fridge for 30 minutes to rest.

9. Brush top of pie with eggwash. Place on a baking tray. Bake for 20 minutes. Reduce heat to 180°C (350°F, Gas Mark 4). Bake for a further 20 minutes or until filling bubbles and pastry is golden. Cool in dish for 10 minutes.

FRENCH APPLE TART

INGREDIENTS

Pastry

1¼ cup (155g, 5oz) plain flour

½ tsp salt

60g (2oz) butter, chilled and chopped

2 tbsps sugar

1 tsp iced water

2 egg yolks

½ tsp vanilla essence

Filling

6 cooking apples, sliced

1 tbsp water

½ cup (110g, 4oz) caster sugar plus 1 tbsp extra

2 tsps vanilla essence

30g (1oz) butter

2 cooking apples, very finely sliced

1 tsp lemon juice

Glaze

½ cup (180g, 6oz) apricot jam

1 tbsp water

METHOD

1. Sift flour and salt into a large mixing bowl. Add butter and rub lightly into flour using fingertips. Continue until mixture resembles fine breadcrumbs, then stir through sugar. Add the remaining ingredients and combine, bringing the dough together with hands.

2. Turn onto a well-floured board. Knead lightly, form into a ball and wrap in plastic wrap. Place in the fridge to chill for 30 minutes.

3. Preheat oven to 190°C (375°F, Gas Mark 5) and grease a 20cm (8in) flan tin. Roll out pastry and place in the base of the tin. Prick with a fork and return to the fridge to chill for 10 minutes until firm. Line with baking paper and blind bake for 10 minutes. Remove the paper and weights, reduce oven to 180°C (350°F, Gas Mark 4) and bake for 10 minutes or until the crust is pale golden. Remove and cool in tin.

4. Place apples in a saucepan with water, sugar, vanilla and half the butter. Cover and cook over a low heat for 20 minutes, stirring until tender. Turn up heat and boil, stirring, until a thick pulp forms. Taste and add more sugar if needed. Spread into the cooled pastry shell.

5. Sprinkle finely sliced apples with lemon juice and sugar. Arrange slices on top of the cooked apple. Melt the remaining butter and brush over the apple. Bake for 30 minutes or until apples are soft and golden brown.

6. Heat jam and water in a saucepan over low heat and stir until dissolved. Pass through a sieve, then return to the pan and bring to the boil. Cook until thickened.

7. Place cooked tart onto a wire rack or serving dish and brush with the apricot glaze. Serve warm or cold.

EASY ORANGE TARTLETS

INGREDIENTS

Tartlets

2 sheets frozen shortcrust pastry, thawed

2 tsps cornflour

1 tbsp water

¾ cup (165g, 6oz) caster sugar

125g (4oz) butter, chopped

½ cup (125ml, 4fl oz) orange juice, strained

4 eggs, lightly beaten

1 tbsp finely grated orange zest

Icing sugar, for dusting

Candied orange zest

1 orange, zested

½ cup (110g, 4oz) caster sugar

⅓ cup (100ml, 3½ fl oz) water

METHOD

1. Preheat oven to 200°C (390°F, Gas Mark 6). Lightly grease a 12-hole muffin tin.

2. Using a cookie cutter, cut twelve 7cm (3in) rounds from pastry. Ease pastry rounds into prepared pan. Prick bases with a fork.

3. Place in the oven and bake for 10 minutes until golden. Remove and set aside to cool.

4. Place cornflour in a small bowl with water and blend until smooth. In a saucepan on medium heat, combine sugar, butter, juice, eggs, zest and cornflour mixture. Bring to the boil, stirring constantly for 5-10 minutes. Reduce heat to low and simmer for 1 minute until the mixture has thickened slightly. Transfer mixture to a heatproof bowl. Cool slightly then cover bowl with plastic wrap and chill in the fridge for 3 hours until cold and thick.

5. Place orange zest, sugar and water in a saucepan and cook over low heat until sugar dissolves. Stir constantly until mixture starts to bubble. Increase heat to medium-high and boil for 5 minutes, without stirring. Pour into a bowl and leave to cool completely.

6. Remove tart shells from tins. Spoon curd into shells. Chill until ready to serve.

7. Top with candied zest and dust with icing sugar before serving.

PECAN PIE

SERVES 6 ★ PREP 40min (PLUS CHILLING) ★ COOK TIME 55min

INGREDIENTS

Shortcrust pastry

1¾ cups (215g, 7oz) plain flour, sifted

Pinch of salt

125g (4oz) chilled butter, chopped

1 egg, lightly beaten

1 tbsp iced water

Filling

50g (2oz) butter, chopped

1 cup (155g, 5oz) brown sugar

²/₃ cup (230g, 8oz) golden syrup

3 eggs, beaten

1 tsp vanilla extract

2 cups (250g, 8oz) pecans, roughly chopped

4 pecan halves, to decorate

METHOD

1. Combine flour and salt in a large bowl. Add butter and rub into flour mixture using fingertips until fine crumbs form. Make a well in centre of flour mixture. Combine egg and water in a small bowl, then pour into well. Using a round-bladed knife, or hands, stir until mixture just forms a dough.

2. Turn out onto a floured surface and shape into a disc. Wrap in plastic wrap and chill in fridge for 30 minutes.

3. Prepate a 30cm (12in) springform fluted flan tin. Preheat oven to 200°C (390°F, Gas Mark 6). Place dough on a floured work surface and roll out to size, using the base of the tin as a guide. Line tin with pastry using the rolling pin to fold over the tin. Trim and discard excess pastry. Cover and refrigerate for 15 minutes.

4. Blind bake for 20 minutes or until pastry is golden. Remove weights and paper. Reduce oven to 175°C (350°F, Gas Mark 4).

5. Place butter, sugar and golden syrup in a small saucepan over low-medium heat. Cook for 5 minutes, stirring constantly, until butter melts and mixture is smooth. Remove from heat and set aside to cool slightly. Add eggs and vanilla, and whisk to combine. Add chopped nuts and stir well to combine.

6. Add filling into the pastry base and smooth over with a spatula. Press pecan halves in the centre to decorate.

7. Place tin on a tray and bake for 35 minutes or until filling is browned and firm to the touch. Remove from oven and cool in tin.

RASPBERRY CREAM TART

INGREDIENTS

Crust

1 cup (125g, 4oz)
plain flour, sifted

¼ cup (40g, 1½ oz)
cornflour

½ tsp baking powder

¼ tsp salt

140g (5oz) butter,
room temperature

¼ cup (55g, 2oz) sugar

2 tsps orange zest

1½ tsps vanilla extract

⅓ cup (115g, 4oz)
raspberry jam

Filling

220g (8oz) mascarpone
cheese, chilled

½ cup (125ml, 4fl oz)
whipping cream, chilled

⅓ cup (50g, 2oz)
icing sugar

1 tsp orange zest

1 tsp vanilla extract

¼ tsp almond extract

3 cups (350g, 12oz)
fresh raspberries

METHOD

1. Preheat oven to 180°C (350°F, Gas Mark 4). Butter a 23cm (9in) springform tart tin.

2. Combine flour, cornflour, baking powder and salt in a bowl.

3. Using an electric mixer, beat butter, sugar, orange zest and vanilla in large bowl until well combined. Add flour mixture and beat until clumps begin to form.

4. Using hands, gather dough into a ball then flatten into a disc. Press over bottom and up sides of prepared tart tin. Place in the freezer for 15 minutes.

5. Place in oven and bake crust for 25 minutes until golden brown. Remove and allow to cool slightly.

6. Spread raspberry jam over the base of the crust. Bake for 5 minutes. Cool in the tin placed on a wire rack.

7. Place mascarpone, cream, icing sugar, orange zest, vanilla and almond extracts in large bowl of an electric mixer and beat for 2 minutes until peaks form.

8. Spread filling evenly in cooled crust. Place in the fridge to chill for at least 2 hours until firm.

9. Arrange raspberries in circles on top of the filling and garnish with mint.

MINI TREACLE TARTS

INGREDIENTS

Pastry

1½ cups (185g, 6oz) plain flour

90g (3oz) butter, cold and cubed

1 tbsp icing sugar

1 egg, beaten

Filling

½ cup (60g, 2oz) breadcrumbs

¾ cup (260g, 9oz) golden syrup

1 tsp lemon zest

1½ tbsps lemon juice

METHOD

1. Place flour, butter and icing sugar in food processor and pulse until butter starts to form small lumps. Add half the beaten egg and pulse for a few seconds or until the mixture starts to come together. Add more egg if required to bring the pastry together.

2. Remove from processor and roll pastry into a ball, then cover in plastic wrap and transfer to the fridge to chill for 30 minutes.

3. Meanwhile, lightly grease a 12-hole muffin tray with butter.

4. Turn the pastry out on a lightly floured surface and roll to a size large enough to accommodate 12 discs. Cut 12 discs using the bottom of a glass. Press each disc into a hole in the muffin tray.

5. Preheat the oven to 180°C (350°F, Gas Mark 4). Blind bake the pastry for 10 minutes until the base is dry. Remove from the oven and set aside to cool.

6. Place breadcrumbs, golden syrup, lemon zest and lemon juice into a mixing bowl and mix until combined.

7. Spoon 1 tablespoon of the filling into each of the pastry cups and press down to flatten.

8. Place in the oven and bake for 25 minutes until the pastry cases are golden and the filling is toasted.

9. Remove from the oven and leave to cool in the tin.

DESSERTS

SERVES 6-8 ★ PREP 40MIN (PLUS CHILLING) ★ COOK TIME 1HR 10MIN

PASSIONFRUIT CHEESECAKE

INGREDIENTS

1 x 250g (9oz) pkt
plain sweet biscuits

125g (4oz) butter, melted

500g (1lb 2oz) cream
cheese, room temperature

¾ cup (165g, 6oz)
caster sugar

2 tsps lemon rind,
finely grated

2 tbsps fresh lemon
juice

2 tbsps plain flour

5 eggs

½ cup (125ml, 4fl oz)
pouring cream

1 tbsp cornflour

⅓ cup (80ml, 3fl oz) water

170g (6oz) passionfruit
pulp (tinned or fresh)

¼ cup (55g, 2oz)
caster sugar

METHOD

1. Line the base of a 20cm (8in) springform cake tin with greaseproof paper. Secure the base into the tin.

2. Place biscuits in the bowl of a food processor. Process until crushed to a fine crumb. Add butter and pulse until well combined.

3. Shake the biscuit crumb onto the base of the cake tin. Using the back of a spoon, spread and press firmly over the base. Cover with plastic wrap and place to chill in the fridge for 30 minutes.

4. Preheat oven to 160°C (320°F, Gas Mark 3).

5. Using an electric mixer, beat cream cheese, sugar and lemon rind in a large bowl until smooth. Add the lemon juice and flour. Beat until fully combined. Add eggs, 1 at a time, beating well after each addition. Add the cream and beat until well combined.

6. Pour the cream cheese mixture on top of the biscuit base.

7. Place on a baking tray and into the oven. Bake for 1 hour, 10 mins or until the cheesecake is just set in the centre.

8. When cooked, turn off the oven and prop the door ajar. Leave the cheesecake to cool in the oven. Place in fridge overnight to set.

9. Combine cornflour and water in a small bowl. Transfer to a saucepan, and add passionfruit and sugar. Cook over medium heat, stirring, for 2-3 minutes or until the mixture boils and thickens. Set aside to cool slightly. Pour over cheesecake. Place in fridge until set.

BAKED APPLES AND CREAM

INGREDIENTS

2½ cups (460g, 1lb) mascarpone cheese

3 tbsps honey

6 baking apples

4 tbsps walnuts, chopped

4 tbsps hazelnuts, chopped

60g (2oz) butter

Walnut halves, to garnish

METHOD

1. Preheat oven to 200°C (400°F, Gas Mark 6) and grease a deep oven dish with a lid.

2. Place mascarpone and honey in a large mixing bowl and stir to loosely combine.

3. With a sharp knife, remove the top third of the apples and remove the core from each. Filll the cavity with the nuts. Add a knob of butter onto each and replace the top third of the apple. Place the apples into the prepared dish and cover.

4. Place in the oven and bake for 30 minutes until apples are very soft.

5. Remove apples from oven and immediately transfer to a serving dish. Remove the top third of the apple and spoon dish juices and marscapone honey mixture over the top. Replace the apple 'lids' and serve with walnut halves.

SERVES 6 ★ PREP 15MIN ★ COOK TIME 30MIN

HONEY BAKED FIGS

INGREDIENTS

6 whole fresh figs

½ cup (110g, 4oz) sugar

⅓ cup (115g, 4oz) honey

2 tbsps lemon juice

1 cinnamon stick

½ cup (60g, 2oz) pistachio nuts, toasted

METHOD

1. Preheat oven to 180°C (350°F, Gas Mark 4).

2. Cut stems off figs and cut a deep cross on top of each. Place figs into a lidded oven dish.

2. Place 3 cups (750ml, 24fl oz) water in a large saucepan over a medium heat. Add sugar and stir until dissolved. Increase heat and bring to the boil. Stir in the honey, lemon juice and cinnamon stick. Boil the liquid over high heat for 5 minutes until reduced and thickened slightly.

4. Pour syrup over the figs and cover. Place in the oven and bake for 20 minutes until figs are soft. Sprinkle with toasted pistachio nuts to serve.

CHOCOLATE CHEESECAKE

INGREDIENTS

Base

160g (6oz) butter

1 x 250g (9oz) pkt plain chocolate biscuits, roughly broken

½ tsp ground cinnamon

Filling

270g (9oz) dark chocolate, finely chopped

120g (4oz) butter

¾ cup (165g, 6oz) caster sugar

3 eggs

750g (1½ lb) cream cheese, room temperature

2 tbsps cocoa powder

1 tsp vanilla extract

2½ cups (600ml, 20fl oz) sour cream

Cocoa powder, to serve

METHOD

1. Preheat oven to 160°C (320°F, Gas Mark 3). Line a 24cm (9½ in) springform tin with greaseproof paper.

2. Melt the butter in a small pan over medium heat.

3. Place the biscuits, cinnamon and melted butter in the bowl of a food processor and process until well combined.

4. Place the biscuit mix in the tin and press firmly around the base. Cover with plastic wrap and put in the fridge to chill for 30 minutes.

5. Place the chocolate and butter in a heatproof bowl over a saucepan of simmering water and stir for 5 minutes or until just melted. Don't over-melt the chocolate. Reserve ¼ cup (60ml, 2fl oz) chocolate sauce for drizzling.

6. Using an electric beater, beat sugar and eggs in a large bowl until light and fluffy. Add the cream cheese and beat until well combined. Add chocolate, cocoa powder and vanilla and gently fold the mixture together with a metal spoon. Add the sour cream and stir to combine.

7. Pour the mixture on top of the biscuit base and smooth the surface with a spatula. Bake for 1 hour or until just firm in the centre.

8. After 1 hour, turn off the oven but leave cake inside with door ajar, for 2 hours or until cooled completely.

9. Remove from the oven, cover with plastic wrap and place in fridge for 2 hours to chill.

10. When ready to serve, drizzle reserved chocolate sauce over the top of each slice, and dust with extra cocoa powder.

NEW YORK CHEESECAKE

INGREDIENTS

160g (6oz) digestive biscuits

80g (3oz) butter

900g (2lb) cream cheese

1 cup (220g, 8oz) caster sugar

¾ cup (200ml, 7fl oz) sour cream

3 tbsps plain flour

3 eggs, plus 1 egg yolk

2 tsps vanilla extract

METHOD

1. Preheat the oven to 180°C (350°F, Gas Mark 4). Line base of a 23cm (9in) springform cake tin with greaseproof paper.

2. Place biscuits in a plastic bag and crush with a rolling pin to form fine crumbs.

3. Melt butter in a saucepan and add the biscuit crumbs, stirring to combine. Allow to cool slightly and then place in base of cake tin. Spread in an even layer, pushing down to flatten.

4. Bake in the oven for 10 minutes until golden. Remove and allow to cool.

5. Reduce the oven to 160°C (325°F, Gas Mark 3).

6. Meanwhile, beat together cream cheese and sugar in a large bowl until smooth then add sour cream and flour and beat again until combined. Add the eggs one by one, and vanilla essence, beating well between each addition.

7. Pour the cream cheese mix on to the biscuit base. Place in the oven and bake for 45 minutes until cooked. The cheesecake should be set but with a slight wobble, and have a golden tone around the edges.

8. When cooked, turn off the oven and prop the door ajar. Leave the cheesecake to cool in the oven.

9. Once the oven is cool, remove the cheesecake and allow to cool completely in the tin.

SERVES 8 ★ PREP 30MIN ★ COOK TIME 40MIN

STICKY DATE PUDDING

INGREDIENTS

1 cup (160g, 6oz)
dates, roughly chopped

1¼ cups (310ml,
10fl oz) water

½ tsp bicarbonate of soda

60g (2oz) butter, room
temperature chopped

1 cup (155g, 5oz) firmly
packed brown sugar

1¼ cup (155g, 5oz)
self-raising flour

2 eggs

Pecan halves,
to decorate

METHOD

1. Preheat oven to 180°C (350°F, Gas Mark 4) and grease eight metal dariole moulds (or ramekins).

2. Put dates and water in a saucepan over high heat and bring to the boil. Remove from heat. Add bicarb, and stir until dates start to break down. Set aside to cool.

3. Using an electric mixer or hand beater, cream butter and sugar until light and fluffy. Add eggs and beat to incorporate. Add date mixture and stir to combine.

4. Sift flour over the top of the wet mixture and gently fold to combine. Divide mixture evenly between the moulds, filling each two-thirds full.

5. Place moulds in a deep-sided dish. Pour water into the tray until it comes up a third of the side of the moulds.

6. Place in oven and bake for 40 minutes or until a skewer inserted in the centre comes out clean. Decorate with pecan halves and serve with butterscotch sauce.

BUTTERSCOTCH SAUCE

INGREDIENTS

50g (2oz) butter

1 cup (155g, 5oz) brown sugar

1 cup (250ml, 8fl oz) cream

1 tsp vanilla extract

METHOD

1. Combine butter, sugar, cream and vanilla in small saucepan over a low heat and cook, stirring, until butter melts and sugar dissolves.

2. Bring sauce to the boil, reduce heat and bring to a gentle simmer. Simmer for 7-8 minutes or until sauce thickens.

MINI CARAMEL CUSTARDS

SERVES 4 ★ PREP 45MIN ★ COOK TIME 40MIN (PLUS CHILLING)

INGREDIENTS

Caramel

¼ cup (55g, 2oz) sugar

2 tbsps cold water

1 tbsp hot water

Custard

3 eggs

¼ cup (55g, 2oz) caster sugar

1⅓ cups (350ml, 12fl oz) milk

½ tsp vanilla extract

⅓ cup (100ml, 3½ fl oz) whipping cream

Sponge cake

2 eggs

¼ cup (55g, 2oz) sugar

⅓ cup (40g, 1½ oz) plain flour

Pinch of salt

¼ cup (30ml, 1fl oz) whipping cream, warmed

METHOD

1. Preheat the oven to 170°C (340°F, Gas Mark 4). Grease 4 individual ramekins.

2. Put the sugar and cold water in a saucepan on medium heat and cook undisturbed until the sugar begins to melt. Reduce heat to low and stir occasionally until sugar is fully dissolved and syrup is light brown. Add hot water into the caramel and immediately pour into the ramekins.

3. In a medium mixing bowl combine ingredients for the custard together and stir until smooth. Pour custard into the ramekins.

4. Whisk the eggs until light and frothy, then gradually add the sugar until thick ribbons form when dropped off a spoon. Sift the flour and salt over the egg mixture and fold to combine.

5. Combine ¼ cup (60ml, 2fl oz) of egg mixturer and warm whipping cream in a large bowl, and gently fold to combine. Add the egg mixture, and fold to combine into a smooth and thick batter. Pour batter into the ramekins, over the custard.

6. Place ramekins into a deep-sided baking dish, and pour boiling water into the dish until it is three-quarters full.

7. Place in the oven and bake for 40 minutes or until the cakes spring back to touch.

8. Remove from the oven and allow to cool completely in the dish, then refrigerate for 4 hours.

9. Run a knife around the edge of the ramekins then turn onto serving plates.

SUMMER FRUIT CHEESECAKE

INGREDIENTS

250g (9oz) pkt plain sweet biscuits

125g (4oz) butter, melted

3 tsps gelatin powder

¼ cup (60ml, 2fl oz) boiling water

500g (1lb 2oz) cream cheese, room temperature

½ cup (110g, 4oz) caster sugar

1 tsp vanilla bean paste (or vanilla extract)

300ml thickened cream, whipped

1½ cups (150g, 5oz) blueberries, fresh or frozen

¾ cup (150g, 5oz) strawberries, fresh or frozen

METHOD

1. Line a deep 20cm (8in) round springform tin with greaseproof paper.

2. In a food processer, pulse biscuits until mixture resembles fine breadcrumbs. Add butter. Process until just combined.

3. Press mixture over base and side of prepared tin. Refrigerate for 20 minutes or until firm.

4. Sprinkle gelatin over boiling water in a heatproof jug. Whisk with a fork until dissolved. Set aside to cool for 15 minutes.

5. Using an electric mixer, beat cream cheese, sugar and vanilla until smooth. Add gelatin mixture and beat until combined. Fold in whipped cream.

6. Pour mixture into prepared tin. Smooth top with a spatula. Cover and refrigerate overnight.

7. Remove cheesecake from tin and transfer to a plate. Pile blueberries and strawberries atop the cheesecake in centre. Garnish with mint leaves and serve.

RHUBARB APPLE CRUMBLE

INGREDIENTS

Filling

4 apples, peeled and cut into chunks

¼ cup (60ml, 2fl oz) water

½ bunch rhubarb, trimmed and roughly chopped

⅓ cup (70g, 2½ oz) caster sugar

Crumble

½ cup (60g, 2oz) plain flour

90g (3oz) chilled butter, chopped

½ cup (80g, 3oz) brown sugar

¼ cup (20g, ¾ oz) shredded coconut

¼ cup (20g, ¾ oz) rolled oats

¼ cup (30g, 1oz) pecans, chopped (optional)

½ tsp ground cinnamon

METHOD

1. Preheat oven to 180°C (350°F, Gas Mark 4). Lightly grease a medium ovenproof dish.

2. Place apple and water in a saucepan over high heat and bring to the boil. Reduce heat to medium, cover and and simmer for 5 minutes, until almost tender.

3. Add rhubarb and sugar into saucepan and simmer for a further 4 minutes, stirring ocassionally, until rhubarb is just tender. Strain and discard any excess liquid. Spoon mixture into prepared dish.

4. Sift flour into a medium mixing bowl. Rub in butter using fingertips until mixture is the consistency of fine breadcrumbs. Mix through the remaining crumble ingredients. Scatter the crumble evenly over fruit.

5. Bake for 30 minutes, until the fruit bubbles and the crust is golden. Serve warm with ice cream.

BREAD AND BUTTER PUDDING

INGREDIENTS

500g (1lb) day-old bread, sliced

2 cups (480g, 1lb 2oz) sultanas

85g (3oz) mixed peel

2 tbsps mixed spice

1 tbsp orange peel (optional)

½ tbsp ground cinnamon

2½ cups (625ml, 20fl oz) milk

2 eggs, beaten

²/₃ cup (100g, 3oz) light brown sugar

100g (3½ oz) butter, melted

METHOD

1. Heat the oven to 170°C (340°F, Gas Mark 4) and grease a glass baking dish.

2. Place bread, sultanas, mixed peel, mixed spice, orange peel, if using, and cinnamon in a large mixing bowl. Pour in the milk and stir well with a wooden spoon, until the bread breaks down.

3. Add eggs and sugar and stir to combine. Stir in the melted butter. Leave to stand for 5 minutes to allow the bread to soak up all of the ingredients.

4. Stir and pour into the baking dish. Add extra sultanas on top.

5. Place in the oven and cook for 1 hour until golden brown on top.

SERVES 10 ★ PREP 20MIN ★ COOK TIME 1HR 30MIN
MIXED BERRY PAVLOVA

INGREDIENTS

4 egg whites

1¼ cup (275g, 10oz) caster sugar, sifted

½ tsp white vinegar

1 tbsp cornflour

2 cups (500ml, 1pt) whipped cream

2 cups (250g, 8oz) mixed fresh berries

METHOD

1. Preheat oven to 200°C (390°F, Gas Mark 6) and line a baking tray with greaseproof paper.

2. Using an electric mixer, beat the egg whites on a medium setting until soft peaks form.

3. With the machine running on high, add the sugar all at once and beat the mixture for 1-2 minutes until glossy. Continue to beat on high until the mixture thickens. When dropped back into the bowl, the mixture should sit on top rather than collapse back into itself.

4. Reduce the mixer to a medium speed and the vinegar. Beat for 10 seconds and then remove the bowl from the mixer.

5. Sift cornflour over the egg white mixture and lightly combine with a spatula.

6. Spoon meringue onto the prepared tray and quickly mould it into desired shape.

7. Place the tray in the middle of the oven and turn the temperature down to 120°C (250°F, Gas Mark ½). Bake for 1 hr and 30 minutes checking before the end that the pavlova has not browned. When cooked, the crust should be firm and the inside soft and marshmallowy.

8. Cool to room temperature and decorate with whipped cream and fresh berries.

PROFITEROLES WITH CREAM AND CHOCOLATE SAUCE

INGREDIENTS

Pastry

85g (3oz) unsalted butter

¾ cup (200ml, 7fl oz) cold water

½ tsp sugar

1 cup (125g, 4oz) plain flour

Pinch of salt

4 eggs, beaten

Cream filling

2½ cups (625ml, 20fl oz) whipping cream

1 tbsp icing sugar

Chocolate sauce

200g (7oz) milk or dark chocolate, broken into pieces

15g (½ oz) butter

1 tsp vanilla extract

4 tbsp water

METHOD

1. Preheat the oven to 200°C (400°F, Gas Mark 6). Line a baking tray with greaseproof paper.

2. Place butter, water and sugar into a large saucepan over a low heat. When butter is melted, increase heat and stir in flour and salt. Remove from heat and quickly beat the mixture until it forms a smooth paste. Transfer the mixture into a large bowl to cool for 10-15 minutes.

3. Add half the egg mixture and stir vigorously until the paste is smooth and glossy. Add more egg until the mixture has a soft dropping consistency.

4. Dip a teaspoon into some warm water and use it to spoon out teaspoons of the dough onto the baking tray.

5. Place in the oven and bake for 30 minutes, until golden brown.

6. Lightly whip the cream and icing sugar until soft peaks form.

7. Melt the chocolate, butter, vanilla and water in a heatproof bowl over a pan of boiling water. Stir contantly until the chocolate is smooth and shiny.

8. When the profiteroles are completely cooled, cut them in half and spoon cream into the middles.

9. Arrange the profiteroles on a serving dish and pour the hot sauce over top to serve.

LEMON DELICIOUS

INGREDIENTS

50g (2oz) butter,
room temperature

¾ cup (165g, 6oz)
caster sugar

3 eggs, separated

⅓ cup (60ml, 2fl oz) lemon
juice

2 tsps lemon rind,
finely grated

½ cup (60g, 2oz)
self-raising flour

1 cup (250ml, 8fl oz)
milk

Icing sugar, for dusting

METHOD

1. Preheat oven to 160°C (325°F, Gas Mark 3) and grease a baking dish with butter.

2. Using an electric mixer, beat butter and ½ cup (110g, 4oz) sugar until light and fluffy. Add egg yolks, one at a time, beating well after each addition. Add lemon juice and lemon rind and mix until combined. Sift flour over and add milk. Using a metal spoon, gently fold to combine.

3. In a separate bowl, beat egg whites until soft peaks form. Add ¼ cup (55g, 2oz) sugar and beat until thick and glossy.

4. Gradually fold egg whites into lemon mixture until combined. Spoon mixture into prepared dish. Place dish in a deep baking tin. Pour boiling water into baking tin to come half way up the sides of the dish.

5. Bake for 45 minutes until pudding has risen and top is golden. Remove from the oven and stand for 5 minutes before removing dish from water. Dust with icing sugar.

CARAMEL DUMPLINGS

INGREDIENTS

Syrup

1 cup (155g, 5oz)
brown sugar

2 tbsps butter

1½ cups (375ml, 13fl oz)
water

Dumplings

1¼ cups (155g, 5oz)
flour, sifted

1 tsp baking powder

½ tsp salt

3 tbsps vegetable
shortening (or butter)

¼ cup (55g, 2oz) sugar

⅓ cup (80ml, 3fl oz)
milk

METHOD

1. Preheat oven to 180°C (350°F, Gas Mark 4).

2. Place brown sugar and butter in a saucepan over medium heat and cook, stirring frequently, for 5 minutes or until just caramelised. Add water and boil for 2-3 minutes. Transfer syrup to a shallow baking dish.

3. Meanwhile, combine the flour, baking powder and salt in a bowl. Rub in the shortening (or butter) with fingertips until the mixture resembles rough breadcrumbs. Add sugar and stir to combine. Add milk and stir gently to form a soft dough.

4. Form dough into balls and drop into the caramel syrup. Place in the oven and bake for 25 minutes.

MINI MERINGUES

INGREDIENTS

4 egg whites, at room temperature

½ cup (110g, 4oz) caster sugar

¾ cup (120g, 4oz) icing sugar

Few drops of rose food colouring

METHOD

1. Preheat oven to 110°C (230°F, Gas Mark ¼) and line two baking trays with greaseproof paper.

2. Using an electric mixer or hand whisk, beat the egg whites until soft peaks form.

3. Increase speed and gradually add sugar, a tablespoon at a time. Continue beating for 20 seconds between each addition. Continue beating until the mixture is thick and glossy.

4. Sift one third of the icing sugar over the mixture, and gently fold it in with a large metal spoon. Continue to sift and fold in the remaining icing sugar a third at a time until the mixture is full and fluffy.

5. Transfer half of the mixture into a fresh bowl and add food colouring.

6. Transfer the mixture to two piping bags with a spiral attachment. Pipe spirals of meringue onto baking tray until all mixture has been used. If you don't have a piping bag, use a spoon to do this.

7. Bake for 1 hour and 15 minutes until the meringues sound hollow when tapped underneath.

8. Remove from oven and leave to cool on the trays.

CHOCOLATE SOUFFLE

INGREDIENTS

Melted butter, to grease

4 tbsps caster sugar

30g (1oz) butter

2 tbsps plain flour

²/₃ cup (160ml, 5fl oz) milk

150g (5oz) dark chocolate, chopped

3 eggs, separated

METHOD

1. Preheat oven to 180°C (350°F, Gas Mark 4). Brush six souffle dishes with melted butter and sprinkle with 1 tablespoon sugar.

2. Melt butter in a saucepan over medium heat. Add flour and stir for 1 minute or until mixture is smooth and begins to bubble. Reduce heat to low, and gradually add milk, stirring until combined. Return to medium heat and stir until mixture thickens and comes to the boil. Boil for 1 minute, stirring. Remove from heat.

3. Add chocolate and remaining caster sugar until combined. Transfer to a bowl. Add egg yolks and stir until well combined.

4. Using an electric beater, whisk egg whites for 5 minutes or until firm peaks form.

5. Fold one-third of the egg whites into chocolate mixture using a metal spoon. Fold in remaining egg whites until just combined.

6. Spoon mixture evenly into the dishes. Place on a baking tray. Place in the oven and bake for 20 minutes or until well risen.

BREAD

PUMPKIN BREAD

INGREDIENTS

1 medium pumpkin,
peeled and cubed

1½ cups (185g, 6oz)
flour

1 tbsp pumpkin seeds

½ tsp of salt

1 cup (220g, 8oz) sugar

1 tsp bicarbonate of soda

1 tsp ground ginger

½ tsp ground cinnamon

½ tsp ground nutmeg

½ tsp allspice

125g (4oz) butter, melted

2 eggs, beaten

¼ cup (60ml, 2fl oz)
water

2 tsps molasses
(or golden syrup)

1 tsp orange zest

½ cup (60g, 2oz)
chopped pecans or
walnuts (optional)

Pumpkin seeds,
to decorate

METHOD

1   Roast or boil pumpkin in a saucepan over a high heat until tender. Puree and measure 1 cup (225g, 8oz).

2.   Preheat the oven to 180°C (350°F, Gas Mark 4).

3.   In a large bowl, combine flour, pumpkin seeds, salt, sugar, bicarb, ginger, cinnamon, nutmeg and allspice. Set aside.

4.   In a separate bowl, mix together pumpkin puree, melted butter, eggs, water, molasses and orange zest.

5.   Add dry ingredients to wet ingredients and stir until just combined. Stir in the chopped nuts, if using.

6   Grease a 20 x 10 x 7cm (8 x 4 x 3in) loaf tin. Pour the batter into the tin and smooth the top with a spatula. Sprinkle with pumpkin seeds.

7.   Place in the oven and bake for 50 minutes or until a skewer inserted in the centre comes out clean.

8.   Remove from oven and allow to cool in the tin for 5 minutes. Loosen loaf from tin by inserting a metal spatula around the sides. Invert tin to remove loaf. Transfer to a wire rack to cool completely.

OLIVE AND BASIL FOCACCIA

INGREDIENTS

1¼ cups (310ml, 10fl oz) warm water

2 tsps dry yeast

2 tsps caster sugar

2 tbsps olive oil

3 cups (375g, 12oz) plain flour

½ tsp salt

1 tsp sea salt flakes

1½ tbsps fresh basil leaves

20 mini roma tomatoes

METHOD

1. Combine the water, yeast, sugar and olive oil in a small bowl. Set aside in a warm place for 5 minutes or until frothy.

2. Place flour and salt in a bowl. Make a well in the centre and pour in yeast mixture. Stir until combined, then use hands to bring the dough together.

3. Turn onto a lightly floured surface and knead for 10 minutes until smooth and elastic. Brush a bowl with oil to grease. Place dough in bowl and cover with plastic wrap or a damp tea towel. Set aside in a warm place for 45 minutes or until doubled in size.

4 Preheat oven to 200°C (400°F, Gas Mark 6) and grease a deep-sided baking tray.

5. Punch down centre of the dough with your fist. Turn onto a lightly floured surface and knead for 2 minutes or until dough is elastic and has returned to original size. Press into the prepared tray. Cover with a damp tea towel and set aside in a warm place to prove for 20 minutes.

6. Press holes into the dough using a spoon or your thumb. Brush with olive oil and sprinkle over sea salt. Press the tomatoes into the dough with a basil leaf underneath.

7 Place in the oven and bake for 30 minutes or until golden brown. Remove from the oven and serve immediately.

BANANA LOAF

INGREDIENTS

3 bananas, medium ripe, mashed

2 tbsps golden syrup

¼ cup (55g, 2oz) caster sugar

1 egg, beaten

1 cup (125g, 4oz) self-raising flour, sifted

Pinch of salt

1 tbsp cinnamon sugar

METHOD

1. Preheat oven to 180°C (350°F, Gas Mark 4) and line the base of a standard loaf tin with greaseproof paper.

2. Mash bananas in a medium sized bowl. Add golden syrup and stir to combine. Stir in the caster sugar and mix thoroughly. Add egg, flour and salt and mix until just combined.

3. Pour mixture into loaf tin and dust lightly with cinnamon sugar.

4. Bake for 30 minutes or until a skewer inserted in the centre comes out clean.

SERVES 10 ★ PREP 40MIN (PLUS PROVING) ★ COOK TIME 35MIN

POPPY SEED ROLL

INGREDIENTS

1 cup (90g, 3oz)
poppy seeds

⅓ cup (80ml, 3fl oz)
boiling water

¼ cup (30g, 1oz)
almond meal

½ cup (110g, 4oz)
sugar

½ tsp vanilla

½ lemon, zested

½ orange, zested

2 cups (250g, 8oz)
plain flour

2 tsps active dry yeast

¼ cup (55g, 2oz) sugar

½ tsp salt

⅔ cup (160ml, 5fl oz)
milk, warmed

2 tbsps vegetable oil

1 egg

1 egg, beaten
(egg wash)

METHOD

1. Grind the poppy seeds in a spice grinder. Transfer to a medium-sized bowl and add water, almonds, sugar, vanilla, lemon and orange zests. Stir and set aside.

2. In the bowl of an electric mixer, combine flour, yeast, sugar and salt. Stir in milk, oil and egg and beat for 2-3 minutes or until a dough forms.

3. Cover dough with plastic wrap and let sit in a warm place for 25 minutes. Line a baking tray with greaseproof paper.

4. Roll the dough into a rectangular shape. Spread filling almost to the edges, and roll from the long end. Seal edges and tuck ends under. Place on baking tray and leave to rise for an hour until doubled in size.

5. Preheat oven to 180°C (350°F, Gas Mark 4).

6. Brush roll with egg wash and sprinkle with poppy seeds. Bake for 35 minutes or until golden brown.

SERVES 8 ★ PREP 15MIN ★ COOK TIME 45MIN

BANANA AND PECAN BREAD

INGREDIENTS

2 cups (250g, 8oz)
self-raising flour

⅓ cup (50g, 2oz)
brown sugar

1 cup (125g, 4oz)
pecans, coarsely
chopped

1 tsp bicarbonate
of soda

2 large ripe bananas

2 eggs, whisked

1 cup (250ml, 8fl oz)
milk

METHOD

1. Preheat oven to 180°C (350°F, Gas Mark 4)°C. Line base
   and sides of a loaf tin with a 20cm (8in) base in greaseproof
   paper.

2. Sift the flour into a large mixing bowl. Add sugar, pecans
   and bicarb, and stir thoroughly to combine.

3. In a medium bowl, mash bananas with a fork.

4. Add eggs, milk and banana, and gently fold until well
   combined. Spoon mixture into the lined pan.

5. Place in the oven and bake for 45 minutes or until a skewer
   inserted into the centre comes out clean.

6. Set aside to cool completely. Cut into slices to serve.

ZUCCHINI BREAD

SERVES 8 ★ PREP 25MIN ★ COOK TIME 45MIN

INGREDIENTS

3 cups (375g, 12oz) plain flour

2 tsps baking powder

¼ tsp bicarbonate of soda

1 tsp cinnamon

¼ tsp nutmeg

1 tsp salt

2 eggs

1 cup (220g, 8oz) sugar

½ cup (80g, 3oz) brown sugar, packed

¾ cup (185ml, 6fl oz) olive oil

2 tsps vanilla extract

2-3 zucchinis, grated and squeezed of excess moisture

METHOD

1. Heat the oven to 180°C (350°F, Gas Mark 4). Grease two 20 x 10 x 7cm (8 x 4 x 3in) loaf tins.

2. Combine the flour, baking powder, bicarb and spices in a large mixing bowl.

3. In a separate bowl, whisk together the eggs, sugars, olive oil and vanilla extract.

4. Stir the zucchini into the flour mixture. Pour the wet mixture over the top. Gently stir and fold until flour is just fully combined. Divide the batter between the two loaf pans.

5. Place in oven and bake for 45 minutes, until golden brown and a skewer inserted in the centre comes out clean.

6. Remove from oven and allow to cool in tin for 5 minutes and then turn onto a wire rack to cool completely.

HERB FOCACCIA

INGREDIENTS

½ cup (125ml, 4fl oz) olive oil

2 garlic cloves, minced

1 tbsp chopped fresh thyme (or 1 tsp dried thyme)

1 tbsp chopped fresh rosemary (or 1 tsp dried rosemary)

¼ tsp black pepper

1 cup (250ml, 8fl oz) warm water

2¼ tsps active dry yeast

½ tsp honey

2½ cups (310g, 10oz) plain flour

1 tsp salt

METHOD

1. In a medium saucepan combine olive oil, minced garlic, thyme, rosemary and black pepper. Cook over low heat for 7-10 minutes until aromatic, stirring ocassionally. Set aside.

2. In a large bowl, stir the warm water, yeast and honey together. Leave to stand for 5 minutes. Next add 1 cup (125g, 4oz) of flour and ¼ cup (60ml, 2fl oz) of garlic-infused olive oil mixture. Stir 3 to 4 times until the flour is soaked through. Leave to stand for another 5 minutes. Stir in remaining flour and the salt.

3. Bring the dough together with your hands and then transfer to a floured surface. Knead the dough for 2 minutes until smooth but don't over-work. Transfer to a large oiled bowl and cover with a warm, damp towel. Leave to rise in a warm place for 1 hour.

4. Preheat oven to 230°C (445°F, Gas Mark 8). Line a rimmed baking tray with greaseproof paper.

5. Transfer dough to the baking tray then press it down into the tray creating the desired shape. Using a sharp knife, slash the dough diagonally several times and then drizzle with the remaining garlic-olive oil mixture.

6. Let the dough rise for 20 minutes until it rises slightly then bake for 20 minutes or until golden brown. Remove from the oven and serve immediately.

HONEY NUT LOAF

INGREDIENTS

1 cup (155g, 5oz)
brown sugar

110g (4oz) butter

1½ cups (185g, 6oz)
plain flour

½ cup (125ml, 4fl oz)
milk

1 tsp vanilla extract

½ tsp baking powder

¼ tsp bicarbonate of soda

Pinch of salt

2 eggs

2 cups (250g, 8oz) coarsely
chopped pecans

Honey, for drizzling

Pecan halves,
for decoration

METHOD

1. Preheat oven to 180°C (350°F, Gas Mark 4). Butter and flour a
    loaf tin and set aside.

2. Using an electric mixer, cream brown sugar and butter until light
    and fluffy. Add flour, milk, vanilla extract, baking powder, bicarb,
    salt and eggs and mix on low speed until combined. Fold in half
    the chopped pecans.

3. Pour batter into prepared tin and bake for 50 minutes, until
    golden brown on top and a skewer inserted in the centre comes
    out clean. Cool cake on a wire rack.

4. Drizzle cake with 1 tablespoon of honey. Scatter the remaining
    chopped pecans and the pecan halves evenly on top, and drizzle
    with another 1-2 tablespoons of honey. Slice and serve.

SERVES 10 ★ PREP 15MIN ★ COOK TIME 50MIN

RASPBERRY BANANA BREAD

INGREDIENTS

150g (5oz) butter,
room temperature

1 cup (155g, 5oz)
brown sugar

2 eggs, lightly beaten

2 very ripe bananas,
mashed

2 cups (250g, 8oz)
self-raising flour

1 tsp baking powder

½ cup (125ml, 4fl oz)
milk

½ cup (60g, 2oz) fresh
or frozen raspberries

METHOD

1. Preheat oven to 180°C (350°F, Gas Mark 4). Line base and sides of a loaf tin with a 20cm (8in) base with greaseproof paper, leaving an overhang on the sides.

2. Using an electric mixer, cream butter and sugar until light and fluffy. Add eggs, 1 at a time, beating well after each addition. Stir in banana.

3. Sift flour and baking powder over banana mixture. Add milk. Stir with a metal spoon until combined. Gently fold in the raspberries.

4. Spoon mixture into loaf pan and smooth the surface with a spatula. Bake for 50 minutes or until a skewer inserted in the centre comes out clean.

5. Remove from oven and cool in tin for 10 minutes. Transfer onto a wire rack to cool completely.

CHRISTMAS GINGERBREAD LOAF

INGREDIENTS

150g (5oz) butter, plus extra to grease

1 cup (155g, 5oz) soft dark brown sugar

½ cup (180g, 6oz) golden syrup

¾ cup (200ml, 7fl oz) milk

2 cups (250g, 8oz) plain flour

1 tsp ground cinnamon

1 tsp ground ginger

1½ tsps baking powder

2 eggs, beaten

¾ cup (90g, 3oz) pecans, roughly chopped

3 pieces candied ginger, chopped

2 apples, peeled and chopped into chunks

METHOD

1. Preheat the oven to 180°C (350°F, Gas Mark 4). Grease and line a 22 x 13cm (10 x 5in) loaf tin.

2. Melt the butter, sugar and syrup in a small saucepan. Once melted, add the milk and stir to combine. Set aside to cool.

3. Sift the flour with the dry spices and baking powder into a bowl. Make a well in the centre and pour in the cooled milk mixture. Using a metal spoon, slowly incorporate the flour until all mixture is moist. Fold through the beaten eggs, pecans, ginger and apples.

4. Pour the mixture into the loaf tin and bake in the oven for 50 minutes or until a skewer inserted in the centre comes away clean. Cool for 5 minutes in the tin, then remove to a wire rack before serving.

FRENCH CROISSANTS

INGREDIENTS

5 cups (625g, 1lb 4oz) plain flour

⅓ cup (70g, 2½ oz) sugar

1 tsp salt

20g (¾ oz) dry yeast

½ cup (125ml, 4fl oz) warm water

500g (1lb 2oz) chilled butter

1 egg, beaten

METHOD

1. Place the flour, sugar, salt and yeast in a mixing bowl. With a wooden spoon, gradually mix in water until a kneadable dough forms.

2. Turn dough onto a lightly floured surface and knead until elastic and smooth. Place dough back in bowl. Cover and chill in refrigerator for 50 minutes.

3. Roll dough into a rectangle. Roll out chilled butter into a smaller rectangle, around 1cm (½ in) thick. Place this in the middle and centre of the dough.

4. Fold each side of the dough over the butter, forming a layer of dough on the bottom, a layer of butter, then two layers of dough. Wrap dough in plastic wrap and chill in refrigerator for 1 hour.

5. On a lightly floured surface, roll dough to a rectangle. Repeat the folding process, folding the long sides into the middle. Return the dough to the fridge for an hour.

6. Repeat this process two more times, then wrap the dough in cling film and let it rest overnight.

7. Using a rolling pin, roll out the rested dough to 3mm (⅛ in) thick. Cut the rolled out dough into squares and cut each square diagonally, making triangles.

8. Place the dough triangles on a lightly floured surface. Roll the croissant and curl it around into the familiar crescent shape.

9. Place croissants on baking trays lined with greaseproof paper and leave to rise for 1½ hrs.

10. Preheat the oven to 200°C (400°F, Gas Mark 6).

11. Brush croissants with egg and place in oven to bake for 15 minutes until golden brown.

CRANBERRY LOAF

INGREDIENTS

2 cups (250g, 8oz)
plain flour

1 cup (155g, 5oz) brown
sugar, tightly packed

1½ tsps baking powder

½ tsp bicarbonate of soda

1 tsp salt

60g (2oz) butter,
melted

1 egg, lightly beaten

¾ cup (185ml, 6fl oz)
milk

3½ cups (350g,12oz)
cranberries, fresh
or frozen

METHOD

1. Preheat oven to 180°C (350°F, Gas Mark 4). Grease and lightly flour a 20 x 10 x 7cm (8 x 4 x 3in) loaf tin and set aside.

2. In a large bowl, combine flour, brown sugar, baking powder, bicarb and salt. Set aside.

3. In a medium bowl, combine butter, egg and milk.

4. Add wet mixture to dry mixture and stir well to combine. Add cranberries and fold well.

5. Pour batter into prepared loaf tin. Bake for 1 hour or until a skewer inserted in the centre comes out clean.

6. Cool in tin for 30 minutes. Invert onto a wire rack, then turn right side up to cool completely.

LEMON LOAF

INGREDIENTS

125g (4oz) butter

1 cup (220g, 8oz) sugar

2 eggs

½ cup (125ml, 4fl oz) milk

1½ cups (185g, 6oz) plain flour

1 tsp baking powder

½ tsp salt

1 lemon rind, finely grated

METHOD

1. Preheat oven to 180°C (350°F, Gas Mark 4). Grease and lightly flour a 20 x 10 x 7cm (8 x 4 x 3in) loaf tin and set aside.

2. In a large bowl, cream butter and sugar until light and fluffy. Add eggs, one at a time, beating after each addition. Add milk and beat to combine.

3. In a large mixing bowl combine flour, baking powder, salt and lemon rind.

4. Add wet mixture to dry mixture and stir well to combine.

5. Pour batter into prepared loaf tin. Bake for 55 minutes or until a skewer inserted in the centre comes out clean.

6. Remove from oven and cool in pan for 5 minutes. Transfer to a wire rack and allow to cool completely.

FRUIT AND NUT COFFEE LOAF

INGREDIENTS

1 cup (160g, 6oz)
pitted soft dates

1 cup (250ml, 8fl oz)
hot coffee

1 tsp vanilla paste
(or extract)

125g (4oz) butter

1¼ cups (195g, 6½ oz)
soft light brown sugar

2 eggs

1¾ cups (215g, 7oz)
self-raising flour

1 tsp baking powder

1 tsp ground cinnamon

¼ tsp ground ginger

½ tsp ground nutmeg

½ cup (60g, 2oz)
pistachio nuts, chopped

½ cup (80g, 3oz)
dried cranberries, chopped

METHOD

1. Preheat oven to 180°C (350°F, Gas Mark 4). Line a 20 x 10 x 7cm (8 x 4 x 3in) loaf tin with greaseproof paper.

2. Put dates in a small bowl and pour over the hot coffee and vanilla. Leave to sit for 20 minutes.

3. Meanwhile, using an electric beater cream butter and sugar together in a mixing bowl. Add the eggs and whisk until smooth.

4. In a separate bowl, combine flour, baking powder and spices.

5. Drain the dates but retain coffee mixture. Add coffee mixture to the creamed butter, sugar and eggs. Whisk until combined, adding a little of the flour mixture to prevent curdling if required.

6. Fold in the remaining flour and spices with a large metal spoon.

7. Finely chop soaked dates and add to cake mixture along with pistachios and cranberries. Stir the mixture until well incorporated and a smooth, glossy batter forms.

8. Bake for 30 minutes or until a skewer inserted into the centre comes out clean.

ORANGE CINNAMON SCROLLS

INGREDIENTS

Dough

2 cups (250g, 8oz)
self-raising flour

Pinch of salt

90g (3oz) butter,
chopped

²/₃ cup (160ml, 5fl oz)
milk

Filling

120g (4oz) butter,
room temperature

4 tbsps soft brown
sugar

2 tsps cinnamon
sugar

2 tbsps orange peel, grated

Coarse sugar,
to decorate

METHOD

1. Preheat oven to 210°C (410°F, Gas Mark 6).

2. Sift flour and salt into bowl. Add butter and rub into flour with fingertips until a rough crumble forms.

3. Make a well in the centre and gradually add milk. Mix lightly with hands to form a soft dough. Add more milk if needed.

4. Knead dough on a lightly floured surface until smooth. Roll out dough to a rectangle of 5mm thickness.

5. Using a hand mixer, beat butter with brown sugar and cinnamon sugar until light and fluffy. Spread evenly over the dough. Spread orange peel over dough.

6. Roll up dough from the long side and slice into 3cm (1in) pieces. Place scroll pieces onto baking tray.

7. Place in oven and bake for 10 minutes until golden.

8. Decorate with coarse sugar before serving.

CHEESY HERB 'CRACK BREAD'

INGREDIENTS

110g (4oz) butter, melted

2 garlic cloves, minced

½ tsp salt

2 tsps fresh parsely, finely chopped

2 tsps rosemary, chopped

2 tsps fresh thyme, finely chopped

1 crusty sourdough or artisan loaf

¾ cup (90g, 3oz) shredded mozarella cheese

METHOD

1. Preheat the oven to 180°C (350°F, Gas Mark 4).

2. Combine the butter, garlic, salt, parsley, rosemary and thyme in a small bowl.

3. Cut the sourdough or artisan loaf on a diagonal both ways to form a diamond pattern. Don't cut all the way through.

4. Prise the cracks open and drizzle butter mixture in between along with the shredded cheese. Wrap the loaf in foil and place on a baking tray.

5. Place in the oven and bake for 15 minutes until the cheese has melted. Remove foil and return to the oven to bake for another 5 minutes until golden brown and crusty. Serve immediately.

SERVES 8 ★ PREP 30MIN (PLUS PROVING) ★ COOK TIME 25MIN

TOMATO ROSEMARY FOCACCIA

INGREDIENTS

15g (½ oz) fresh yeast

3 tbsps warm water

1¾ cups (215g, 7oz) plain flour

2 tsps fresh rosemary, finely chopped

4 tbsps olive oil

1 garlic clove, crushed and mixed with 2 tbsps olive oil

12 to 15 cherry tomatoes

Sea salt

METHOD

1. Preheat the oven to 180°C (350°F, Gas Mark 4).

2. Mash the yeast with the water and leave it for 10 minutes to go frothy.

3. In a large bowl, mix the flour with some salt and 1½ teaspoons rosemary. Reserve the leftover rosemary for garnishing. Make a hollow and stir in the yeast mixture, then the oil and mix to form a soft dough. Turn the dough out on to a lightly floured surface and knead for about 10 minutes until it is smooth and elastic.

4. Cover the bowl with a clean tea towel and leave in a warm, draught-free place for 1 hour until it has doubled in size.

5. Turn out on to a lightly floured surface and knead lightly. Roll out to form a circle about 6mm (¼ in) thick.

6. Place the dough circle on a lightly oiled baking tray and brush with the garlic oil. Make indentations with your finger and put a tomato in each. Bake for 25 minutes or until golden brown.

7. Remove from oven and leave to cool slightly on a wire rack. Sprinkle with sea salt and reserved rosemary. Serve warm or cold cut into triangles.

POTATO ROSEMARY BREAD

INGREDIENTS

1 sachet (7g, ¼ oz) dry yeast

1 tsp sugar

1 cup (250ml, 8fl oz) lukewarm water

4 cups (500g, 1lb) plain flour

½ tsp salt

3 tbsps olive oil

3-4 white potatoes, very finely sliced

150g (5oz) feta

2 tbsps lemon juice

Salt and pepper

2 tbsps rosemary leaves

METHOD

1. Mix yeast and sugar together and sprinkle on top of lukewarm water. Rest for 10 minutes or until frothy.

2. Mix flour and salt in a mixing bowl. Make a well in centre and add the dissolved yeast mixture and olive oil. Combine well with a wooden spoon.

3. Turn dough onto a floured surface and knead until smooth. Cover with plastic wrap or a damp tea towel and rest for 45 minutes.

4. Blanch potatoes in boiling water for 5 minutes or until just tender.

5. Preheat the oven to 180°C (350°F, Gas Mark 4).

6. Place dough on a floured work surface and knead for 3-4 minutes before rolling out into a rectangle, with the middle thinner than the edges. Place on a baking tray lined with a baking paper.

7. Mix feta, lemon juice, salt, pepper, potato slices and rosemary and spread on top.

8. Place in the oven and bake for 15 minutes until golden brown.

INDEX

HERRON
book distributors PTY LTD

First Published in 2016 by Herron Book Distributors Pty Ltd
14 Manton St
Morningside
QLD 4170
www.herronbooks.com

Captain Honey
WWW.CAPTAINHONEY.COM.AU

Custom book production by Captain Honey Pty Ltd
PO Box 155
Byron Bay
NSW 2481
www.captainhoney.com.au

Cataloguing-in-Publication. A catalogue record for this book is available from the National Library of Australia

ISBN 978-0-947163-09-9

Printed and bound in China by Shenzhen Jinhao Color Printing Co., Ltd

5 4 3   17 18 19 20

NOTES FOR THE READER

Preparation, cooking times and serving sizes vary according to the skill, agility and appetite of the cook and should be used as a guide only.

All reasonable efforts have been made to ensure the accuracy of the content in this book. Information in this book is not intended as a substitute for medical advice. The author and publisher cannot and do not accept any legal duty of care or responsibility in relation to the content in this book, and disclaim any liabilities relating to its use.

PHOTO CREDITS